INVISIBLE
FRONTIER

INVISIB
FR

L. B. DEYO &
DAVID "LEFTY" LEIBOWITZ

THREE RIVERS PRESS
NEW YORK

LE

EXPLORING

THE TUNNELS,

RUINS, AND ROOFTOPS

OF HIDDEN

NEW YORK

ONTIER

Published by Three Rivers Press, New York, New York

Member of the Crown Publishing Group, a division of Random House, Inc.
www.randomhouse.com

THREE RIVERS PRESS and the Tugboat design are registered trademarks of Random House, Inc.

Printed in the United States of America

DESIGN BY ELINA D. NUDELMAN

Library of Congress Cataloging-in-Publication Data is available upon request.

ISBN 0-609-80931-8

10 9 8 7 6 5 4 3 2 1

First Edition

THIS BOOK IS FOR PETER GRAFF, A MAN OF ADVENTURE,
AND FOR
CHAMPION, A MOST LOYAL BEAST

Jinx has ceased its unlawful trespassing activities for the duration of the present period of war and heightened alert in the United States; though neither odious nor evil, the activities of urban exploration create the hazard of false alarms and could potentially divert police resources from serious matters. Obedience of just laws is not a private matter. Every crime undermines our safety by making the staggering task of law enforcement harder in this period of terrorism and war.

Jinx, New York City, April 2003

CONTENTS

ACKNOWLEDGMENTS

Jinx magazine is more than a publication. It is a family of writers, editors, and designers, a crew of explorers and adventurers, and an arena for discussion and debate. Since its first issue in 1996, the magazine has relied on the talents and energy of its all-volunteer staff. Without their efforts, the magazine that inspired this book would not have been possible. Our heartfelt thanks, then, to *Jinx* magazine senior editor Jeff Wilson; contributing editors Sir Ellis, D., and Dan Weisberg; publisher Joey Edwards; associate publishers Mary Deyo and Christina Deyo; cartoonists Buzz Moran, Lance Fever, Carolyn Kelley, and Walt Holcomb; art directors Sandi "Q" Quatrale and Eleanor Renée Rogers; designers Slim Golomb, Miriam Blankenship, Eric Lundquist, and crsthaDISH; marketing director Françoise Evanchik; publicists Dinha Kaplan and Michelle Eccevarria; poet laureate Speed Levitch; photographers Shaul Schwarz, Josh Weinfeld, Stacia Murphy, Jefferson Richard Keyton, and Daniel Arsenault; models Pandora, VirtuaVal, and Jamie; and writers Eric Bleich, S. Morgan Friedman, Denver Smith, Eric "the Butcher" Grostic, Jeremy Fulton, Chris Standish, Dhyana Kuhl, Oliver Green, Jon Connors, Aaron Mindel, Julia, Ninjalicious, Commodore Brett Smith, KMD, Scott Sala, Kevin White, Syntax Era, David Sergenian, Gus Peña, Ken Grobe, and Lara "Dr. No-No" DeNonno.

The explorations undertaken for this book required the talents and expertise of many *Jinx* agents. We gratefully acknowledge the work of Agent Bleach (Eric Bleich), Agent Gage (Sara Gage), Agent Née (Eleanor Renée Rogers), Arch-Agent Gabriel (Aaron Mindel), The Brain (Michel Evanchik), Steve Duncan, Agent Brazen, Nick Science, Agent Illich (Chris Snyder), Salamander X (Scott Sala), and the photographers and reporters who joined us. These brave explorers risked their lives and dignity for the Jinx Project.

The brilliant and distinguished Chris Jackson has been far more than an editor to us, having conceived of the book, approached us, guided us through the whole publication process, shaped the manuscript, and fought for us whenever we needed him. Our excellent agent, Daniel Greenberg, has been an invaluable ally and advocate. We wish to thank the entire Three Rivers staff, especially Melissa Kaplan, Brian Belfiglio, Elina D. Nudelman, and the human dynamo Tracy Kuehn.

For love, support, and inspiration the authors wish also to thank Eleanor Renée Rogers, Jerm Pollet, Noah "Homeslice" Genel, George "Lurp" Murr, Leigh Anne Jackson, Benny "Burrito" Webster, Roger Brown, James Morel, Jacqui Barcos, John Painter, Noah Max Shachtman, Helin Topdagi, Mark Nineteen, Blacktongue, Presto Augustus, Kathleen Hulser, Stephen Williams, Todd Seavey, Arielle Jamil, Alix Spiegel, William B. Deyo, Jr., Valerie Merin, Kathleen Deyo, Frank Perelli, Mary Deyo, Christina Deyo, Mary Catherine Orr, Ruth Ann Waite, Peggy Waite, Paul Orr, Nancy Orr, Jean Deyo,

Pam and John Lucca, Debbie and Geoffrey Howe, Russell and Stephanie Deyo, David and Colleen Deyo, Donald Deyo, William B. Deyo, Sr., Emily Fromm, Bobby and Adrian Leibowitz, Patricia Doyle, John Caligiuri, Stanley London, Mildred Doyle, Tamara Goheen, the Ramblin' Kings, Matt Owens, Chepo Peña, Space Commander Stefan Jackson, Marcy Shoemaker, and all the brave souls of the urban exploration movement.

FOREWORD

In 1996, L. B. (Laughing Boy) Deyo and I created *Jinx*, the magazine of Worldwide Urban Adventure. In it, we published articles about exploration of the city's infrastructure, from climbing to the tops of bridges, to spending twenty-four hours in the subway system, to searching abandoned Air Force bases. Soon we began to receive correspondence from other urban explorers all over the world. We had stumbled upon a burgeoning community. A New York–based urban exploration group called Dark Passage had gained notoriety for staging a four-course meal in an abandoned subway tunnel in Brooklyn. Ninja-licious in Toronto had created the first handbook for the urban exploration movement with *Infiltration, the Zine About Going Places You're Not Supposed to Go*. We heard about people kayaking through storm drains in Minnesota, swimming in submerged catacombs in Paris, and mapping out abandoned ruins in Australia. The press began to call, and features on *Jinx* and urban exploration (known as UE for short) appeared in the *New York Times, Seattle Weekly, Details, Artbyte, New York Magazine,* the Associated Press, and on National Public Radio.

For this book, L.B. and I spent three months in intensive explorations of New York, beginning in the deepest places and working our way to the highest. Either L.B. or I narrate each chapter. Our goal was to capture the heart of urban exploration, from our tales of adventure in the city's guts to the history and personalities that make our strange avocation so rewarding.

Lefty Leibowitz

A wonderful fact to reflect upon, that every human creature is constituted to be that profound secret and mystery to every other. A solemn consideration, when I enter a great city by night, that every one of those darkly clustered houses encloses its own secret; that every room in every one of them encloses its own secret; that every beating heart in the hundreds of thousands of breasts there is, in some of its imaginings, a secret to the heart nearest it!

Charles Dickens, *A Tale of Two Cities*

NEW YORK CITY stands anchored in five-hundred-million-year-old igneous bedrock, in compressed strata of shale and stone. Since the seventeenth century this bedrock has been dug, entrenched, drained, tunneled, and blasted to accommodate the roots of a growing infrastructure. As of the summer of 2001, the streets conceal a labyrinth 780 miles in area, and over eight hundred feet deep.

Four hundred forty-three miles of train tracks carry the subways and commuter trains beneath New York. Cars access the city through twenty-two tunnels.

Three hundred forty-six miles of aqueducts and six thousand miles of water mains and tunnels carry 1.5 billion gallons of water beneath the city each day. Most of the city's water mains were built before 1930, and they fail at a rate of 90.11 breaks per one thousand miles per year.

Seven hundred and fifty thousand manholes access the utility grid. New York City power runs through 83,043 miles of underground cable, enough to encircle the globe three and a half times. Thirty-three thousand underground transformers step down the charge for consumer use. One hundred six million telephone calls connect each day through New York's one hundred million miles of telephone cables, which, if stretched end to end, could reach the sun.

HELL:
THE DEEP PLACES
PART I

ONE

LEVIATHAN:
THE CROTON AQUEDUCT

<table>
<tr><td rowspan="12" style="writing-mode: vertical-rl;">Attach label, or print or type</td></tr>
</table>

Attach label, or print or type

Mission
CROTON AQUEDUCT, EARLY SUMMER 2001

Location
THE BRONX

Goal
TO WALK TO MANHATTAN FROM THE BRONX, UNDERGROUND

Officers
LEFTY LEIBOWITZ, L. B. DEYO

Team
GAGE, SPECIAL AGENT RENÉE, AGENT BLEACH, THIAGO
EL ROJO, BRAZEN, NICK SCIENCE, SALAMANDER X

REPORTED BY ▼

L. B. Deyo

L. B. Deyo

And as I stared through that obscurity,
I saw what seemed a cluster of great towers,
whereat I cried, "Master, what is this city?"

Dante, *The Inferno*

IN THE SHADOWS of the city waits an invisible frontier—a
wilderness, thriving in the deep places, woven through
dead storm drains and live subway tunnels, coursing
over third rails. This frontier waits in the walls of abandoned tenements, it hides on the rooftops, and it infil-
trates the bridges' steel. It's a no-man's-land, fenced off
with razor wire, marked by warning signs, persisting in
shadow, hidden everywhere as a parallel dimension.
Crowds hurry through the bright streets, insulated by the
pavement, never reflecting that beneath their feet lurks a
universe.

EXPELLED

From the sidewalk, I hobble into fluorescent glare. Muscle spasms strum across my back; tendons snag like
they're caught in a zipper. It's two A.M. I'm in a Twin
Donut in the Bronx.

I raise a forearm to shield my eyes from the fluorescent
lights, grab a chair, and sit. Seven agents follow me into
the shop, back to the land of the living. Nobody smiles.

"Nick," I call out. "Who invented these lights? Fluorescent lights?"

Nick takes his place in the doughnut line, looking like I
feel, splattered mud drying on his glasses. "Fluorescent

lights." He nods, screwing in his face. "*Tesla* invented them. Nikola Tesla."

"Nikola Tesla." I slump toward the floor. My tie's too tight, strangling me, but I can't get it loose. I'm shivering. Sweat beads on my forehead, with the grime. "Damn the son of a bitch. *Nikola Tesla.* Tinkering bastard." I can't sit still, can't even bend my legs. I get up and take a place in line.

Pain forks through me, forcing my eyes shut. Visions burst across my eyelids, hypnagogic phantoms like the ones you see when you're trying to fall asleep. I see tunnels diminishing to blackness.

I open my eyes and only then do I notice the customers aren't eating. It's late, and there aren't many people here besides us, maybe eight or nine seated throughout. Every one of them is frozen, open-mouthed, staring at us.

"Excuse me," a woman says. She's having a cigarette, sitting with her friend at the table next to me. She's a little drunk, a little bleary-eyed, but she seems all right.

"Yes?"

"Do you mind if I ask"—the woman leans in slightly and blinks twice—"what you all been *doing*?"

Fair question. Here are eight agents fresh from the trenches, in a North Bronx Twin Donut Shop, wearing sunglasses at two in the morning on Puerto Rican Day. The men wear suits and ties; the two women wear cocktail dresses. Several of us have miners' helmets or headlamps. We're encrusted with mud and crystalline mineral deposits, and our shoes have lately been underwater.

"We were exploring the Old Croton Aqueduct," I tell her, "the original New York water supply line. It runs right beneath here."

"For *real?*" She squints. "You all look like a bunch of lawyers."

THE BODY

> For by art is created that great LEVIATHAN called a COMMONWEALTH, or STATE (in Latin, CIVITAS), which is but an artificial man, though of greater stature and strength than the natural, for whose protection and defense it was intended; and in which the sovereignty is an artificial soul, as giving life and motion to the whole body.
>
> **Thomas Hobbes,** *Leviathan*

Social structures form at every level of scale, from the country village to the multinational corporation, from the conversation in a doughnut shop to the transcontinental alliance. Of all these structures, none is fitter, more adaptive, than the city.

It's a macrocosm of the human body, living through its anatomical processes. Its immune system attacks infection through police and emergency workers. Its circulatory system pumps goods throughout the marketplace in huge arteries; these fan out in every direction, branching into finer vessels and capillaries. The nerves of the city pulse with signals, animating, electrifying, communicating, and uniting millions of differentiated cells into an organism. As in a human, these systems are mostly automatic. Without the direction of a central executive, the city breathes and sweats, consumes and excretes.

Nikola Tesla understood that a place can be a living thing. Tesla was the inventor of the Tesla coil, an amplifier of electrical charge. With the Tesla coil he ionized the very air into a conductor, closing the circuit of a current to a slingshot loop, ramping up the voltage by a thousand times, which manifested itself in the slithering arc seen in Frankenstein laboratories. In 1899 Tesla built his largest coil, atop a two-hundred-foot tower, in the skies of Pikes Peak, Colorado. The Jovian engine came alive, hurling lightning bolts in every direction. It inspired the RKO Pictures logo and blacked out the city of Colorado Springs.

For months before he built the tower, Tesla spent his hours measuring the summit's inherent charge. He concluded that the earth itself was "literally alive with electrical vibrations." The tower's genius was to tap into the conductivity of the mountain. Rather than generate power, Tesla's tower would derive it as an antenna receives its radio signal, passively accepting the system's energy. The result was the greatest electrical discharge yet harnessed by man, and it split the night sky.

Few modern cities benefit from Tesla's wisdom. In design, they squander natural vitality. Today's urban planners, impatient with growth and infatuated by theories, impose the limits of their own imaginations. They build soulless, congenitally defective abominations: Los Angeles; Phoenix; Houston; Toronto; Celebration, U.S.A. Failed experiments, bereft of life.

On the other hand, there is New York. The Empire City was designed as a simple grid, ensuring long vistas and fluid movement. As the blueprint came to life, and construction proceeded up the island, the grid worked as the lattices of a fence, allowing wild growth of vines and ivy through a loose and simple matrix. Like the interlocking pattern of Tesla's tower, the grid plan bridged the gap between the artificial order and natural chaos, shaping and focusing an explosion of energy. Over the centuries, the city has evolved into a New World Leviathan. Operation C-1609 would be Jinx's journey through the living body of New York.

The plan was laid out as a list of targets, each a badlands outpost, each offering its own empirical promise. We would proceed upward from the depths, from the intestine labyrinths of the aqueducts and subway lines, through condemned buildings and landmarks, up into the bridges and rooftops until we reached the top of the antenna on One World Trade Center, at more than 1,726 feet the closest place to heaven in New York.

For the first mission of our operation, Jinx set out to probe the city's guts, marching down into the mouth of New York. In the geometry of the tunnels we sought an evolutionary snapshot, a fossil record in progress. The goal was to explore as much of New York's water intake and drainage as we could without drowning. As water moves through the five boroughs, it mostly runs in prohibitively cramped steel pipes. To get our feet wet, we'd want the aqueducts that bring fresh water from up north, tunnels you could drive a car through. We picked the Old Croton Aqueduct because it was semiretired. We assumed it would be pretty empty. We knew we could get in and had hopes of getting out as well.

Were we ready? I harbored grave self-doubts. Captain Sir Richard Francis Burton, by the time he found the source of the Nile in 1858, spoke twenty-seven languages, had been ordained in the Islamic and Hindu faiths, and was the finest swordsman in Europe. I didn't even have a library card. The Age of Exploration was gone; we of Jinx had never breathed its vigorous air. Ours was not the compass, the machete, or the duel, but the mouse, the flip-flop, and the Casual Friday. We sprang from a whited epoch of online chat rooms, grade inflation, and psychic friends; years of Thinking Globally while Acting Locally, of asking What Would Jesus Do?; it was a time of Lollapaloozas, Promise Keepers, and vegan airline meals. Instead of virtue we had correctness; instead of fighting we signed petitions. We had no love affairs, only relationships; no safari, only Earth Day; no death, only recycling. Where were honor, courage, guts, and style? Consigned to the classics section of the video store. An anemic generation cowed through faddish decades, growing softer and more churlish, waiting for a battle cry. The cry, when it came, was "Mean People Suck." How could we be ready?

DOWN THE RABBIT HOLE

Mission One, nine P.M. A trail leads right from the sidewalk into the woods of Van Cortlandt Park. We've been following that trail for close to an hour now. The dusk paints its rich line of blue behind the trees. We walk at the crest of an embankment that drops off sharply on either side, twenty feet down into darkness.

We've got a big team. Jinx usually goes out in twos and threes, but for this reconnaissance Lefty and I assembled a unit of eight, our largest-ever command.

Agent Bleach, the backbone of Jinx security, was the first man we called. Bleach, as anyone can see at a glance, is not human. His ghastly pallor, penetrating stare, and jet-black widow's peak mark him as nocturnal, and so he is: He sleeps by day, often at his desk, and by night creeps through a sticky undergrowth of East Village drug bars. Like the vampire he emulates, Bleach appears ethereal yet owns a terrible reserve of strength and endurance. Imagine your own worst night of chemical and sexual indulgence, then imagine living it *every* night and rising every morning afterward with the sun to face a full day of work. Bleach was made for this mission.

To flatter my scientific aspirations, we called in Brazen and Nick Science. Brazen is an editor at *Scientific American,* a specialist in planetary science, and a graduate of the Cornell program at Ithaca, where his office had been one floor above Carl Sagan's. By his manner, speech, and face alike, Brazen projects an appealing gentleness. Here is a man serious, mature, self-effacing, good-humored, and wise—therefore alien to us, therefore to be closely watched. Nick is a theoretical chemistry graduate student at Columbia, fluent in quantum sorcery. Like Brazen, he seemed inexplicably modest, a thoroughgoing gentleman. Presumably he was feigning. We had the brains of the operation.

The eyes would belong to Renée and Gage, our photographers. Pro-strength shooters, formally trained, they knew the challenge waiting for them in the tunnels. Natural light is never known there, and we'll squeeze no studio lights down the rabbit hole; flashbulbs, ruinous to composition, must suffice. Gage is tall, with shocks of blood-red hair falling across a Cleopatra gaze. Renée is an alabaster nymph in astonishing curves, black hair straight down to the small of her back, eyes liquid, lips engorged. Their alarming beauty, and the levity of their *condescension* to our serious work, must discomfit every man on the team.

Walking behind them is a new agent, little known to us. He is Thiago El Rojo, a Brazilian national working in New York. Rojo had approached us through the Web, and I had been impressed with his digital artistry. He was a mystery to us otherwise; he seemed to be a political radical and was certainly highly intelligent. We're not so simple as to trust a foreigner, naturally, but in the open and liberal spirit of the Jinx Project, we brought him along.

Our oldest protocol forbade any reasonable safety measures, maps, preparation, or planning. For this mission we made an exception: We allowed ourselves a guide. This was Scott Sala, known to his peers as Salamander X.

Scott's a handsome kid. He turns the ladies' heads. Strong build, broad shoulders, dark hair and eyes. He's a movie-star type; he wears the suits and shades well. *How I hate him.* Great chin. They call him the Casanova of Cavers. They call him Don Juan in Hell.

Salamander's never really at home unless he's crawling through the frigid blackness under ninety feet of rock. His free time is for tearing off to the Northeast's toughest caves, most of them uncharted. He's linked up with a network of kindred souls and holds rank and title in the local Caver hierarchy. The avocation is primeval. Sal and his fellow cavers (they save the term *spelunker* for the amateurs they must constantly rescue) lower themselves into three-hundred-foot shafts, swim blind through flooded caverns searching for the next air pocket, and microblast their way through rock to get at virgin caves. Success, for Sal, is busting into a tunnel that's been sealed shut since the age of mastodons, leaving footprints through the dust of twenty thousand years.

"Here it is," says the Salamander as we reach a concrete gatehouse. It's a bland structure, two stories high, ghostly in the failing light. The graffiti crews have been at it. The gatehouse is one of many along the aqueduct; they controlled the water flow and provided access for repairs. This one has no doors or windows, but it's supposed to be our way in. "We'll enter down there." Salamander points his flashlight down the slope of the embankment at a stream that flows out the side. "There's a drainpipe that's just big enough to crawl through."

As we regroup at the bottom, Salamander takes the lead. He crawls in headfirst, feeding himself to New York. The pipe admits his body, while spitting out a stream of runoff beneath him. He's dressed uniquely in the annals of caving: high boots and utility belt, headlamp and two spare flashlights, black suit, navy silk shirt, black tie, and sunglasses. The Jinx uniform is sacrosanct, and permits no modification whether at cocktails or in dank sewers. It's the line we draw between the squares and us.

I take a deep breath and follow. The pipe fits like a straightjacket, flooded and crowded with bramble from the forest floor. I balance on the slick rocks, struggling to keep clear of the water. I'm struggling to stay dry, knowing I'm going to get wet, knowing that before I emerge from the manhole hours from now my suit will be soaked in mud and silt and petroleum byproducts.

My hand slips and plunges wrist-deep into the stream. "Water's cold!" I shout back to the others, who wait around the entrance to follow. I can't expand my chest enough to take a breath. For a moment I freeze. The urge to escape is strong, but I can't turn around. *Could I crawl backward if I had to?* I close my eyes and let the feeling wash through me.

"This is where we climb into the gatehouse," Salamander calls from twenty feet ahead. He's standing, showing me only his boots; there's obviously some sort of an opening overhead. By the time I reach it, he's climbed up and out of the pipe. The opening is a kind of well, leading up into the structure. Salamander sits on the ledge of the well, looking down at where I stand at the bottom, some twelve feet below. From some dark fold on his person he produces a yellow canvas strap, which he ties to a pipe and lowers down to me.

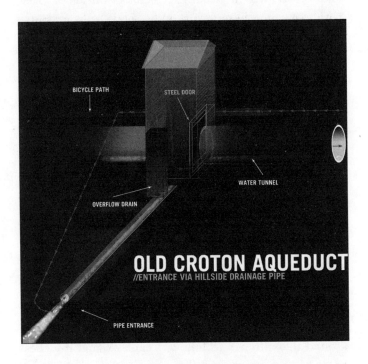

BICYCLE PATH

STEEL DOOR

WATER TUNNEL

OVERFLOW DRAIN

OLD CROTON AQUEDUCT
//ENTRANCE VIA HILLSIDE DRAINAGE PIPE

PIPE ENTRANCE

One by one, the Jinx agents traverse the pipe and reach the well. One by one, Salamander and I help the agents climb up the strap and into the gatehouse. Now all inside the building, we let our flashlights rove over its spartan interior. No skylight, no ornament, just the rusted gears of an ancient engine. It smells like peat and wet leaves. In the center of the room lies a flooded depression, flanked on either side by steel doors. These are the floodgates that controlled the flow of water to Manhattan. The doors are old, but solid, probably half a ton in mass. There's a twelve-inch gap between the door's bottom edge and the concrete floor. This clearance allows a minimal water flow, an emergency vent for high-pressure buildup. Right now just a putrid trickle runs through it.

Salamander tells us matter-of-factly that this gap is our entrance to the aqueduct and asks who will squeeze through first.

Special Agent Renée volunteers. She drops to her belly, in her black strapless evening dress and rain slicker, and squeezes her way under to the other side of the door. Five minutes later, we're all through, standing at last inside the Old Croton Aqueduct.

A BURIED HISTORY

Our flashlight beams crisscross wildly through the vapor, racing over row upon row of old brick. The air is stale. We're in a cylindrical tunnel, eight and a half feet high, seven and a half feet across, forty-one miles long. The curve of the floor creates a hollow in the center, as in a bottle turned on its side. Through this hollow the water filters slowly along, stewing in the mud and rubbish. This dolorous stream, six inches deep at its center, is all that remains in a tunnel that once conveyed millions of gallons per day.

Sal takes point, hissing orders. Bleach and Thiago take up the rear. We're on our way south, to Manhattan. As my eyes begin to adjust to the darkness, and my feet adjust to the slope of the tunnel floor, I try to see as far ahead as I can—about a hundred feet down a gradient to black. This passageway, entombed beneath the oak and poplar forest, gives little outward sign of its significance. Most New Yorkers have never heard of this place. But without the Old Croton Aqueduct, the New York we know wouldn't exist.

Why they changed it, I can't say
(People just liked it better that way)

The Four Lads

In 1664, Peter Stuyvesant, governor of the Dutch colony New Amsterdam, received a British demand of surrender. His colony was besieged, encircled by warships, but the governor tore up the orders. His defiance never had a chance to ring throughout the Empire, however, because the colonists literally pasted the papers back together and made him sign. New Amsterdam was sick of Stuyvesant's paternalistic laws and tempted by British guarantees of freedom and safety. It was also thirsty.

The city, then as now, suffered a dearth of local fresh water. The East River is no river at all, but an undrinkable tidal strait, part of the Atlantic Ocean. The southern Hudson River, along Manhattan's western shore, is a saltwater estuary. Private wells provided the only drinking water until the first New York reservoir was dug in 1776, on the east side of Broadway between Pearl and White Streets. Another reservoir opened in 1800 on Chambers Street. But these were far from adequate. Private wells became polluted with cholera, typhoid, and yellow fever. There were no sewers. Fire brigades drained the reservoirs, fighting conflagrations that razed whole blocks at a time.

In 1837, workers broke ground in a dam in Croton, New York. The dam created a 36-million-gallon reserve and flooded four hundred acres of farmland, including homes. The courts shouted down landholders' protests. A public project was on, the first major aqueduct of modern times; any property in the way would be bought and seized. There were rivers of concrete to pour, millions of bricks to lay, miles of trenches to dig. Twelve tunnels, linked by bridges and pipes, would carry the water down a gentle grade all the way from Croton Falls to central Manhattan. Four thousand Irish were trucked in and handed shovels—they earned seventy-five cents a day and slept in tents. When they protested about the pay and rough conditions, police put them down, in 1838 and again in 1840.

The father of the aqueduct was John Bloomfield Jervis, the greatest American engineer until the Civil War. Jervis transformed America through his leading role in the canal and railroad revolutions. He took his first job as an Erie Canal axeman in 1817; ten years later he was named chief engineer of the Delaware and Hudson Canal Project. This authority emboldened him to add something new to the project—something to be found nowhere else in the United States: a railroad.

A technology's infancy always favors broad generalization of talent. Jervis exploited the newness of his field, working outside the constraints of modern specialization. He was an inventor (of the standard locomotive truck); a contracting engineer (for the Chenango and Erie Canals, the Boston Water Supply Project, and three different railroads); a superintendent (to the Pittsburgh, Fort Wayne, & Chicago Railway); an economist (author of *The Question of Labor and Capital*), an artist, cartographer, and applied scientist. Of all his achievements, the Old Croton Aqueduct topped the list hands down. This was no mere covered trench. The aqueduct included the Croton Dam; the Ossining Bridge; the Harlem River Bridge; the Receiving, Equalizing and Distributing Reservoirs on Manhattan; and forty-one miles of embankments, tunnels, and arches: all in all, the most ambitious engineering project ever attempted in the Americas.

In 1842 the Crystal Palace Exposition was launched, on 42nd Street, Manhattan. The exposition was modeled after London's Crystal Palace, a kind of prototype for the World's Fair. The palace was colossal, towering over the city with burnished glass to mirror the sun. The theme was progress. New fruits of industry, new technology, new invention, and breakthroughs in science were displayed. The Industrial Revolution was at full steam; Victorian science had discovered the dinosaur and the electromagnetic field, and the daguerreotype and the telegraph were the latest rage, but nothing in the show could compete with the inauguration of the Croton Aqueduct. It was instantly declared a marvel of the world, a paradigmatic triumph. Mark Twain was on hand to describe the scene in a letter to his sister Pamela:

The Latting Observatory (height about 280 feet) is near the Palace—from it you can obtain a grand view of the city and the country around. The Croton Aqueduct, to supply the city with water, is the greatest wonder yet. Immense sewers are laid across the bed of the Hudson River, and pass through the country to Westchester County, where a whole river is turned from its course and brought to New York. From the reservoir in the city to the Westchester County reservoir the distance is thirty-eight miles and, if necessary, they could easily supply every family in New York with one hundred barrels of water per day!

It was apt that the aqueduct should be born at this feast to progress. Water is an order of survival; in resolving that urgent need, New York had removed its last barrier to growth and development. The sudden water wealth attracted a massive influx, exploding the population so quickly that a new Croton Aqueduct was immediately required.

WHERE THE GOBLINS GO

The cylinder of the tunnel is imperfect, being slightly taller than wide, but it's round enough to make walking above the waterline a chore. Every step is a new chance to slip into the drink. Some agents, sporting tall rubber fishing boots, splash noisily down the center of the floor. I alone have chosen style over comfort, to the extent of being too stupid to bring boots at all. Even above the water's edge, there is mud and the floor is slick. Within half an hour I have slipped into the water and flooded my shoes.

Our marching order fluctuates roughly along these lines: Salamander at the front, conversing with Lefty or Brazen. Ms. Gage and Ms. Renée follow closely after, stopping occasionally to snap a picture. Nick Science and I keep pace with each other, more or less. Bleach and Rojo, alert for trouble, guard the rear.

The tunnel curves so gently, and fades into darkness so abruptly, that I must continuously resist the thought that we are about to walk off a cliff. We know the tunnel is on a downhill grade, but it's imperceptibly slight. There are few features to break the monotony. Every few minutes we pass under a manhole or spot a surveyor's writing on the wall.

"The brick is elegant," Renée says, laying her hand against the wall.

In the flashlight glare, the corrosion of the tunnel burns with color. Layers of red clay and milk-white mortar have worn thin, exposing concrete and old granite piling. Renée's right: The place flickers with sepulchral glamour. The interlocking patterns on walls, their endless brick iterations down the funnel of perspective, draw us in. But elegance, as Einstein said, is for tailors. This place owes its beauty not to artists but to engineers.

ANCIENT ENGINEERS

The Roman Empire was in some respects a weak extension of Greek achievement. Roman philosophy was shallow, its mathematics prosaic, its science uninspired. In each of these deficiencies we implicate their distrust of the abstract. Plato's Academe in Greece had championed speculation and intellectual detachment. The Romans sneered at such impractical daydreaming, which to them was effeminate Oriental decadence. Romans favored hands-on problem solving, hard work toward a concrete goal. This prejudice led to the slaying of Archimedes by an impatient legionnaire, but it also led to a particular Roman genius for engineering.

Rome was the first major city in history to be decently supplied with water. This was not due to the Tiber River, which by the time of Augustus had begun, like all urban rivers, to stink. Rome slaked its thirst using a consolidation of inherited technologies, which the Romans applied and improved systematically. The general Marcus Agrippa, during the first century, was ordered to meet the needs of a growing city. He organized the construction of a series of aqueducts. The aqueduct concept was even then old news, at least as old as Jerusalem, but the Romans knew of it solely through their Etruscan predecessors. The need for Roman innovation came from the scale of Marcus Agrippa's task. His aqueducts must span unprecedented distances, across varied ground. Each obstacle in the water's path required a new means of conveyance. Pressurized pipes dipped into valleys, tunnels bored through mountains, and arcades leveled uneven terrain. For most of the way from source to consumer, the favored design was a covered trench. This protected the water from sabotage, theft, and erosion. It was also cheap. The trenches were lined with stone, then concrete was poured, then brick laid. The roof was shaped as an Etruscan arch, which mitigated variations in air pressure.

The Roman water system had its problems. First, lead is poisonous, as they knew, but brass pipes were too expensive. The solution was to use lead, but minimize the extent of its journey each gallon spent in pipes. Second, there was the inevitable creep of chaos into every large project. Trenches had to meet up with tunnels, pipes had to fit into pipes, arcades must be the right length and height, bricks must fit together uniformly. The solution to these problems was administrative, and was provided by Vitruvius. He was a writer, architect, and engineer, known through his great work *De architectura*, published in 40 B.C.

The Old Croton Aqueduct obeys Vitruvius' prescriptions. As we walk down the tunnel, we see what Marcus Agrippa might have seen, surveying his project two thousand years ago. Only the most trivial details—rivets in the manhole covers, soda cans in the mud—appear every half-mile or so to remind us this is not the ancient world. Why did Jervis use the techniques of Agrippa? Why not exploit the intervening science or refer to modern theory? Maybe Americans are like the Romans: We don't like windy theories. We like hands-on problem solving, hard work toward a concrete goal.

WILDERNESS

"What are these?" Lefty picks up a shiny object from the water.

"Candles," says Brazen.

From this desultory point, extending forward into the darkness, little candles line the water at both sides. I can only imagine what they looked like when they were lit. They must have cast a holy light and framed a sacramental path. The air must have choked with sulfur.

Lefty and I exchange a nod. We've got a pretty fair idea who left these candles, but we ain't talking. Half the personnel on this mission are new to Jinx. They aren't cleared for Project secrets. Even if they were, it wouldn't help them to know the truth.

Urban exploration groups are strange, even by extralegal standards. Some are just gangs, busting into condemned hospitals and throwing firecrackers around. Some are crack paramilitary units, raiding active government facilities by stopwatch. The most dedicated explorers work alone. But of all flavors of urban exploration, the most dangerous style is witchcraft. A New York crew, well known to Jinx, has for years conducted occult research in profane spaces like this one. When they're not exploring, they run huge underworld parties. Luring innocents with lighthearted invitations, they trap their guests in deep romantic chasms and perform orgiastic rituals of wine and fear.

I pocket a candle. What the others don't know, they don't need to know. "Candles couldn't have been here long," I say. "One good rain would have raised the water-line, washed them away."

Nobody replies. I see fatigue in the faces around me. The condensation has gotten thicker as we've progressed. Balancing along on the curve has bunched the muscles in my calves. It's hot, but my feet and ankles are freezing.

Gage has her camera out, focused on the ceiling ahead, and she brushes aside her red hair to shoot. Something grazes her head.

"*Shit!*" She steps back in the water, almost losing her footing. "What the fuck is *that*?"

"It's a bat," Rojo says. He ducks down with the rest of us, pressing close to the wall. There it is, too, wheeling for another pass, approaching through the ambient light. It looks like a movie prop bobbing on a string. Doesn't make a sound. Then it's gone.

"*Quick* little bastard," I call after it. How did a bat get in here? Are there more ahead, dangling from the ceiling, pissing ammonia into the once-great water supply? The farther we push into this long grave, the more evidence of contamination confronts us. The outside pushes its way in. Engineering succumbs to environment, the walls oxidize, the trespasser leaves his trash. Wild grass roots grow thicker as we proceed, hanging down from the mor-tar in jeweled webs. How long did it take them to bore down through the soil, to trace the microscopic pores of the brick? Mindless, each tendril has solved the maze and found the vapor, clung and crawled into the tunnel, down into the current to drink.

A crunching sound breaks my reverie—the sound of our footsteps, punching through the mud. Some kind of crust has formed along the water and up the wall in glittering streaks.

"Okay." The Salamander stops short to take command. "We're getting into some crystal formations now. If you don't mind, please refrain from touching the stalactites. Your skin has oils that will stick to the formations and change their patterns of growth."

Salamander warned us ahead of time not to disturb the environment down here. It's probably his standard speech to guests on any cave expedition. In this instance, he needn't have bothered. A Jinx mission has few rules, but keeping the site pristine is one of them. This is a city, not a nature preserve; it is nevertheless a living system and subject to erosion. Future explorers deserve to discover this place and perceive the unbroken links to its origin. What we miss, they might find. We resist the urge to touch. The stalactites glisten white, like icicles in a department store window display. They form from deposits in the soil, Nick tells me, alkaline salts and related minerals. For a quarter mile or so, we're in a pleasure dome with caves of ice.

From the corner of my eye, I catch a glimpse of Bleach. He has never seemed more ghoulish than now, wild-eyed in the fiery glare.

"You okay?" I ask, slowly sidling up to him. I don't know if it's the presence of his bat familiar, the descending mineral spikes, or the spent candles left over from their unholy purpose, but Bleach seems entranced. He startles me with a broad smile. Before I can speak again he says, "Salamander tells me he is an angler in the lake of darkness."

REPULSED

For three more hours we slog down the channel, looking for signs of High Bridge, our crossing to Manhattan. If we can make it all the way, we'll emerge in Central Park. We've had to wade across flooded chambers, carrying our shoes, watching the light bleed from the highway floating on the water's surface. We've passed an inflatable alligator, verifying the legend once and for all. I've tested several escape hatches, each at the top of its own ladder in a hollow of the wall; none has budged. So we proceed with Russian fatalism, one foot before the other.

"How deep is it?" Lefty asks.

He and the others at the front have stopped. I drag my way up to see what's the matter.

"I can't tell," says Salamander X, sounding water with a tree branch. "Pretty deep. I can't feel the floor."

We've reached an obstacle. It's a collection pool, not more than fifteen feet across, separating this leg of the tunnel from the next. It shimmers as he churns the water, which fills the whole compartment. There's no way around or over the pool.

I shudder. This isn't like the other rooms we've crossed; none of them was flooded deeper than a foot. Even then, there were grumbles. When I told the team they'd have to wear the full uniform, few questioned it. We're used to getting our best clothes dirty. But wading through this cold, oily slime is demoralizing, especially when you're trapped underground.

El Rojo, grinning, steps up. "I'll find out how deep it is," he says, flashing those white Brazilian choppers. Hell if he doesn't do it, too; he lowers himself into that evil serum until his shirttails are submerged. In the field, you want to stay dry. It's a fundamental of survival. Once you get wet, you stay that way. But the exuberant El Rojo hasn't transgressed much beyond the rest of us; we're all half-soaked by now. "It doesn't get deeper than this," he says. He's more than waist deep, wading to the far side of the pool, where the next tunnel starts toward Manhattan.

"I think we should turn back," Lefty says. "I'm very skeptical about finding an exit farther down. We could get lost, or we could get stuck."

"There's no way I'm getting in that water with my cameras," Gage says.

I look into the unanimous faces. The people are hurting. They're edging toward claustrophobia, anxious to breathe fresh air. More than anyone, I'm responsible for getting them stuck down here.

"All right," I say. "You want to turn back, we'll turn back. You *gutless, treacherous—*"

Lefty slaps me on the back, hard. "Who else likes Twin Donut?"

I stifle my dissent. We've walked a long time, and covered very little ground. It was naïve to think we'd reach the steel pressure pipes of the High Bridge. It would take days, with no assurance of escape at the end of the line. The retreat is sounded.

PHLEGETHON

> This Divorce between a man and his life, the actor and his setting, is properly called the feeling of absurdity.
>
> **Albert Camus,** *Le mythe de Sisyphe,
> essai sur l'absurde*

The physiological requirements of speech, in cranial capacity and mouth structure, are found in hominid fossils 150,000 years old. Whether these hominids were truly human and spoke is a mystery. The evidence suggests speech arrived much later, during the Upper Paleolithic, around 40,000 B.C. The single best sign that real *Homo sapiens* lived that long ago is the remains of early burial rites. These shape the question of what separates beasts from men.

Apes use tools. Bartering and rudimentary medicine are part of chimpanzee life. But burying the dead, with ceremony and artifacts, may have been the first uniquely human behavior. Funeral rites imply thought, belief in an afterlife, faith in individuality and a soul. The gestures of faith are thus central to our species, evident since the caves of prehistoric Europe. They also suggest an abiding association between death and the earth beneath our feet.

Walking back to the north now, I'm confronted by the archetype. The grade of the floor, so subtle before as we walked downhill, now asserts itself. At every step the mud sucks down my shoes. Scanning the ceiling for some means of escape, I feel colder than before. Like the others, I slouch along, round-shouldered, glassy-eyed, through the footprints of an hour ago. We pass under a seam in the highway and feel the booms thundering through.

"I called my friends before I came down here," Gage says, "so that they'd know what happened to me." She smiles, but nobody else sees it. "Tell the truth, I'd rather die here than be buried in a grave. Here at least there's a little room."

The echo of splashing feet, the crazy dance of flashlights through steam, the hours of unbroken trudging, laboring not to slip into the water, all of it piles up now in the muscles of my neck and shoulders. I'm nauseated.

Odysseus descended to the land of the dead through Persephone's grove and searched for blind Tiresias. Aeneas probed deeper, past unburied souls and the Elm to which False Dreams Cling, to Charon's ferry. Dante found in Hell a hybrid of classical Tartarus and Christian perdition, a monstrous engine of torture. Milton's Prince, flung by God into the lowest darkness, built a city there called Pandemonium.

The deep soil is profane; it rots the bodies of the dead. It's sacred, too, for the rites that usher us off, and the holy stillness we find here. The first Christians hid underground from persecution; singing outlawed hymns in catacombs beneath the streets of Rome. Something else colors this depth, though; something I hadn't found in books, or felt in other tunnels. It's the divorce from reason, the drunken confusion of flickering lights, the upside-down logic here, where we look up at grass roots instead of looking down at grass. We're cut off from the Apollonian sunshine, far below the cool heads of engineers who plan from above.

Bare concrete is the city's comfort, drying footsteps, smoothing over rough ground. The bright streets weave their logic, the sidewalks reassure. The drivers on the highway play their radios, talk into cell phones, hurtle past, and are gone. Buried here far beneath them, we listen.

EMERGENCE

To get back up to the shining world from there
My guide and I went into that hidden tunnel;

And following its path, we took no care
   to rest, but climbed: he first, then I—so far,
Through a round aperture I saw appear

Some of the beautiful things that Heaven bears,
Where we came forth, and once more saw the stars.

Dante, *The Inferno*

Salamander reaches the exit first. Instead of leaving the way we came in, we'll take a shortcut up a two-story silo. It's an athletic route. Drag your ass up the wall onto a six-foot ledge. Scramble from there onto either of two I-beams, then across them to a nasty climb up a narrow manhole—our round aperture—with a missing rung no one remembers to tell you about, up onto the wet grass once more to see the stars.

The night air alone is worth it. We haven't reached Manhattan—in fact, we're back at the same park entrance we passed through hours before—but we've walked an ample swath of the aqueduct, more of which might have proved redundant.

That doesn't mean we're satisfied. In every agent's face I see the hunger to learn more, to press further. That, or they're mad at me.

To hell with them. We've seen the geometry of evolution. Roots filtering through solid walls into the tunnel's dank air, narrowing spikes of salt crystal, forks of lightning in an ionized sky. This is the ambition of dynamic systems, in herd populations or weather fronts, in the branches of trees and the dense linkages of computer networks. An infinite curve, a web of transformations.

Passersby have already begun staring at us as we head for the Twin Donut. Our battered force, staggering proudly from its first battle, steeped in glory. Let the people stare, the damned fools and rollerbladers. They don't know the river that snakes beneath them toward Manhattan. Or the pipes that branch off from that river in every direction, narrowing in a Renard series: each pipe's diameter derived from the previous one's multiplied by the nth route of ten. The pipe routes are uncharted, cloaked in mystery. Our streets conceal a Gordian knot of wires, chutes, conduits, water mains, and power lines. The jungle grows always denser, geometrically more complex, as new pipes are sewn into old gaps, new lines are born and old ones die. The system is alive, adapting, and a wilderness is born, shaped by the very drive that impels us to explore it, too vast and promiscuous ever to be fully known, but always rewarding further searches. This is our frontier, and we've begun.

TWO

ART CRIMES:
THE FREEDOM TUNNEL

Attach label, or print or type

Mission
THE WEST SIDE AMTRAK TUNNEL, JUNE 2001

Location
UNDERNEATH RIVERSIDE PARK

Goal
TO FIND EVIDENCE OF THE CITY'S GREAT GRAFFITI
WRITERS AND TO UNCOVER THE MYSTERY OF THE MOLE
PEOPLE

Officers
LEFTY LEIBOWITZ, L. B. DEYO

Team
SPECIAL AGENT RENÉE, JOSH, STEVE DUNCAN

REPORTED BY ▼

Lefty Leibowitz

Lefty

Well said, old mole. Canst work i' th' earth so fast?
A worthy pioner!

Hamlet, Act I, Scene V

I STAND SWEATING on a dirt ledge in a remote, garbage-littered corner of Riverside Park, far from the crowded bike paths and baseball fields. A pair of train tracks lies directly ahead, at the base of a ledge about ten feet down from where we stand. The tracks run to the south, where a hundred yards off they lead into the huge gaping mouth of a tunnel. L.B., Renée, Josh, and Steve Duncan are at my side, exhausted. We've spent the last half hour trudging through underbrush in the hot sun, searching for this spot.

And now we've found it: the Amtrak tunnel of Manhattan's Upper West Side, used by trains traveling between Grand Central Terminal and destinations to the north. By all accounts, this tunnel superficially resembles the other tunnels we've explored: It's dark and foreboding, and frequented by speeding trains. But this tunnel also has secrets that are completely unknown to commuters.

First, it was the home of a massive homeless "city," complete with electricity and hand-built apartments, chronicled in the book *The Mole People* (Jennifer Toth, Chicago Review Press, 1993) and the film *Dark Days* (2000). When authorities caught wind, the homeless city was destroyed, and the people who lived here moved into public housing. A handful of people managed to avoid expulsion, however, and supposedly still live here today in their underground encampments. Desperate and impoverished, these mole people somehow survive far from the tenements and high-rises of the city above.

Second, the tunnel is an epicenter of New York City graffiti culture. Here, and in other colorfully named locations such as the One Tunnel and the Ghost Yard, the city's most renowned graffiti artists painted. They used to write on subway cars, but when the MTA's "Clean Train Movement" was declared on May 12, 1989, trains that showed any sign of graffiti were no longer allowed to operate. Writers had to find new places to work. The Amtrak tunnel was a two-mile canvas.

For a graffiti artist, a subway car is fundamentally different from the fetid, stinking hole that we are about to enter. A subway car will carry a writer's piece throughout the city, exposing it to tens of thousands in a single day. In this tunnel, no one can see the pieces. Only those few intrepid souls willing to enter, or those unfortunate enough to find themselves here without alternative, can stumble upon them. The writers who painted here toiled in the dark to create art without an audience. The results of their labor go unappreciated. In its purity, the act reminds me of the Tibetan Buddhists who spend weeks creating rice powder mandalas, only to sweep them away immediately after completion.

THE DESCENT

Steve Duncan, an old associate and friend who contributes to *Jinx* magazine, quickly removes a thick nylon strap from his bag and attaches it to a lone metal fence pole, about fifteen feet high, planted alongside the tracks. He's the only one of today's group who's been here before, and now he acts as de facto leader. Resplendent in a dark suit, sunglasses, and dyed red hair, he shimmies down the pole using the strap for leverage, and then crouches down alongside the tracks. One by one, the rest of us follow down the ledge, until we're all standing along the tracks.

From here it's no more than fifty yards to the mouth of the tunnel itself. Inside, the temperature is scalding. Two sets of tracks run through the tunnel, along with a forty-foot strip of earth and gravel running parallel to the west of the tracks. The strip is wide enough for us to walk shoulder to shoulder without getting hit by a passing train. That will work to our advantage: These tracks are active. Trains pass through here every twenty minutes or so as they approach and depart from Grand Central Station, more than a hundred blocks to the south. They will be traveling at top speeds, often over a hundred miles per hour, and won't slow down for darkly attired explorers who linger on the tracks.

We walk forward purposefully, the gravel under our feet crunching and grinding with each step. Fifty yards into the tunnel a patch of light filters down from the ceiling, illuminating the extraordinary amount of graffiti that adorns the walls of the tunnel. Though much of it is in a pedestrian "tagging" style (whereby writers scrawl a stylized signature in marker or spray paint), there are already hints that skilled artists have congregated here. Several signatures are written in an ornate "wild style," a technique that uses more sophisticated colors, outlines, and dynamic lettering.

A SHORT HISTORY OF GRAFFITI

Even though it's been around for as long as mankind, the specific urban strain of modern graffiti that we see here is a relatively recent phenomenon. The sophisticated and extravagant "pieces" (short for masterpieces) that New Yorkers have grown accustomed to seeing around the city started with the trend of tagging, an innovation most often credited to a Washington Heights youth named Taki 183. Taki was a seventeen-year-old who lived on 183rd Street and whose job as a messenger allowed him to travel all across the five boroughs on a daily basis. Taki began writing his name all over the trains and stations of the transit system (mostly in a simple, unadorned marker scrawl), and it wasn't long before people began to take notice. On July 21, 1971, the *New York Times* ran an article titled "Taki 183 Spawns Pen Pals," reporting on the sudden phenomenon of rapidly multiplying tags, and in the process made a folk hero out of Taki.

Of course, the *New York Times* wasn't the only one to notice. All over New York, kids became enamored of the idea of their names traveling across the city, seen by tens of thousands of commuters every day. The lure of fame proved overwhelming, and the trend of tagging grew.

With so many youths competing for attention and space, it soon became necessary to go beyond simply scrawling one's name in black marker on a train wall in order to be noticed. A greater level of originality became valued, as did more ambitious works. Logos, stylistic variations, size, and color were added to make the pieces stand out from the crowd. It wasn't long before writers were covering entire sixty-foot by twelve-foot cars with a single work, a formidable and highly respected accomplishment among graffiti artists. This process of innovation and evolution continues.

This tunnel we are exploring today is known for being the home of impressive graffiti pieces by three artists in particular: Sane, Smith, and Freedom Chris. Although there is a strict Jinx policy against agents writing graffiti during expeditions, we take an archaeologist's view of the elaborate pieces we hope to see today. The most impressive pieces are a key element of the urban landscape and worthy of our notice and study.

Sane and Smith were brothers whose tags could be seen all over the city, including the top level of the Brooklyn Bridge. The city, wanting to make a point, hit the duo with a three-million-dollar lawsuit. It was dropped a short while later when Sane was found drowned in Flushing Bay. Nobody knows if he committed suicide or if he fell accidentally from a nearby bridge while writing. Tags and pieces that include references to the memory of Sane now fill the Amtrak tunnel.

The third writer to make this tunnel famous is Freedom. His murals and masterpieces, as elaborate in technique as they are grandiose in scope, take up entire sections of wall here. His work is so omnipresent that some graffiti writers now refer to the Amtrak tunnel as the Freedom Tunnel.

DANGERS OF SEARCHING FOR THE CITY'S LOST ART

We move from the patch of light and continue forward. Soon, L.B.'s voice shoots through the darkness.

"Train!"

The train is still not visible, but an approaching engine screams a warning as Duncan motions to the rest of the group. We crouch in a niche alongside the far wall, hoping to stay out of sight. It is dark here, but we're still afraid the conductor will spot us. It would be a simple matter for him to radio our presence to the authorities.

Within seconds, the train flies around the bend, throttling by at full speed. The hot air singes my face, and I duck my head into my body to shield my eyes from the mushrooming dust. The roar of the engine is deafening. I peek up to see commuters lining the windows of the train, peacefully reading their newspapers. They are unaware of our presence, and of the transgressive art that sits in the darkness outside their well-lit cabins.

We remain crouched for a full minute after the train passes out of sight, not wanting to take any chances of being seen, and then resume walking south along the tracks. The tunnel is unlit, but every few hundred yards grates on the ceiling allow slices of light to penetrate into the sections below. It is in these sections of light where the most elaborate graffiti resides. The writers have designed these underground galleries so the natural light from the grates illuminates their pieces.

Twenty blocks into the tunnel we encounter a huge mural, about fifty feet long, painted in the American Pop Art style. Preternaturally square-jawed comic hero Dick Tracy shouts, "Drop that gun, mole!" in one panel. Another panel features an all-American family traveling by automobile, with a giant flag in the background and a caption: "The American Way." A third panel reproduces a vintage Coca-Cola advertisement. It is signed only "Freedom."

This is the first piece of Freedom's that I've seen, but I recognize immediately that it is different from the urban tags associated with the classic subway art of the 1970s and '80s. This mural embraces an entirely different ambition—it vibrates with the writer's outlaw energy, but also bears signs of an artist's thoughtfulness, depth, and knowledge of earlier forms.

THE MYSTERY OF THE MOLE PEOPLE

As we continue our walk deeper into the tunnel, I notice debris littered everywhere: Shoes and clothing and other miscellany are piled high. This place was once filled with makeshift dwellings constructed from cardboard and built into the corners and shadows of the tunnel walls. The debris around us is all that's left of those structures. It is our first sighting of what were once homes of the so-called mole people.

Tales of vast colonies of homeless people living in the abandoned subway tunnels of the city have long persisted: fully furnished living rooms complete with electricity, televisions, air conditioners, and cooking facilities; shanties made out of scrap metal, plywood, and sheet plastic, some with occupants who've lived underground as long as twenty-five years. My only personal experience with the underground homeless population has been to stumble on a few small stashes of personal items found hidden away in random subway tunnels: a tennis sneaker, a handbag, a milk crate filled with old newspapers. I have never run across signs of a massive organized presence before. Now that's changed.

According to the book *The Tunnel* by Margaret Morton (Yale University Press, 1995), this location has long been a haunt for the city's homeless. By the time the Hudson River Railroad was built in the mid-1800s, squatters had already occupied the mud flats alongside the water. Before long the community expanded to include a tar-paper shantytown and 125 people, who derived their food from the nearby garbage dumps. When the Depression hit a few years later, the competition for food increased as starving crowds set upon the mounds of filth to grab anything edible before it was carted off to sea.

In the 1930s, the shantytown was bulldozed and the mud flats were covered by a concrete and steel structure, in effect creating today's Amtrak tunnel. The plan was to extend Riverside Park to the water, thereby making the area more attractive to the residents of the expensive apartments nearby. The pollution and smoke from the diesel engines, as well as the smell of pigs and cattle being carted to the slaughterhouses, would be hidden away.

And that's exactly how it happened, until the mid-1970s, when rail service in the tunnel was discontinued due to a lack of profitability. When Amtrak started putting down new tracks in 1991, workers discovered that a new community of homeless had sprung up, this time more than 150 strong. Soon afterward, Amtrak began demolishing the shanties. We now stand amid the wreckage.

"Check it out," L.B. shouts out to us. He is standing alongside a queen-size mattress, several cans of food, and dirty and torn items of clothing. Someone still lives here in the darkness. There are three empty and discarded wallets and a small pink handbag, likewise empty, only a few feet away.

"Everyone be careful with their flashlights. Keep your voices down," Duncan whispers. "We need to be as discreet as possible. We don't want to wake anyone."

I look up as I hear laughter. Two small children are playing near the grate immediately above our heads somewhere in Riverside Park. They are enveloped in shadow, backlit by the rays of the sun that are shining through the grate and into our tunnel. They quickly step away from the grate and their laughter recedes in the distance.

THE UNDERGROUND MUSEUM

We push farther south now, practically tiptoeing. As we walk, I continually glance over my shoulder, surveying the entire length of the tunnel. On most missions, the only threats we face are from inanimate objects. The mole people are probably harmless, but I'd just as soon not conduct any interviews today. Despite attempts to be liberal-minded, I can't shake my retrograde prejudices about those who would live in this urban hell. Images of knife-wielding maniacs and muttering schizophrenics dominate my mind.

About five blocks farther is another piece by Freedom: a lifelike rendering of baseball star Ted Williams, taking up a hundred-square-foot panel. A baseball diamond lies just outside a nearby access point. Was Freedom hoping that the Little League players would catch a glimpse through the darkness? It would be hard for them to see, but it wouldn't be impossible when the light of the setting sun filtered in from the west. It is a strange choice of subject matter for a graffiti artist: another icon of 1940s Americana. If Freedom is trying to make a statement about patriotism and the American dream, I'm not sure what it is. Regardless, his subject matter seems out of place here in this darkened tunnel full of the homeless and other detritus from the mainstream culture. Is his work a critique of American values? Or a stab at post-modernist irony?

Renée has moved fifty yards ahead and is scanning the walls of the tunnel with her flashlight. As she shoots the beam across the western wall of the tunnel, I discern another image in the distance. Walking forward, I see a painting of a bomber-jacketed man with only a spray can for a head, his shoulders slouched forward lazily, his hands stuffed into the pockets of his jacket. It is a self-portrait of Freedom that I've seen reproduced in a book on graffiti, but there's something that's changed since the photos were taken. Someone has written over the piece in pink chalk the words, "I am burning this—Seven."

To write over someone's work is the ultimate act of disrespect in the graffiti world. Violent turf wars among writers and crews have often started with this simple offense. The example before us is particularly egregious, in that a recognized and respected artist like Freedom has been written over by a self-indulgent nobody. The word "toy" means an incompetent or rookie writer in graffiti slang. Whoever this "Seven" is, it is obvious he's a toy trying to gain respect for himself at the expense of his superiors.

As we walk on, more pieces line the tunnel walls: a montage of melting watches, à la Salvador Dali (also by Freedom) and a painting of the Unabomber with the words "this one is for my peoples revs, cost, smith, freedom, twist, and of course espo?" written alongside. These pieces are worthy members of this underground gallery: Their size, detail, and scope rival the others we've seen.

"Let's keep moving," Josh shouts to us. "I want to get out of here."

He looks uneasy and anxious. This tunnel is a claustrophobic's nightmare. Josh is a big, strong guy, with a lot of guts, but the tunnel is hot and dark and filled with speeding, hazardous trains. Only a pinprick of light at the far south end promises hope of escape from the rats and filth.

Duncan pokes his head out from a hole in the western wall of the tunnel and smiles. He is standing in a small alcove above a narrow staircase. To his right is a gated and padlocked fence leading out to a skate ramp in Riverside Park. Just twenty feet away, teenagers practice their jumps and twists on the ramp. He rushes down the stairs and joins us.

The five of us walk quickly through the tunnel now, anxious to make our exit. We've been here for well over an hour now, and the heat, fear, and exhaustion have taken their toll on our psyches as well as our bodies. I keep my eyes focused straight ahead on the light shining in from the tunnel exit ahead. Almost there.

And then I catch sight of it out of the corner of my eye. Spread out across a thirty-foot stretch of wall lies a graffiti re-creation of *Third of May*, Goya's painting of a bloody execution during the 1808 Spanish War of Independence. A man stands across from a firing squad, his arms up in the air. Another man kneels to his right, hands clasped together in prayer and supplication. The mural is stunningly true to the original, though the coloring is more muted and monochromatic than Goya's.

Duncan had told me about the story behind this mural on the way here. Freedom and Smith had come down to the Amtrak tunnel and camped with the homeless for the duration of the piece's creation. They worked on it for days, sometimes employing the help of the locals, sometimes working on their own. When it was completed, Freedom and Smith added a dedication to the memory of Sane. Perhaps that is the reason for the somber color choice. Or perhaps they were sending a message to the people that lived down here: that the artists sympathized with the misery of the mole people's lives. That even in the most degraded circumstances, creativity could thrive.

Whatever their motivation, it was not the same of

those in the mainstream art world. The art in the Amtrak tunnel will never be shown in SoHo galleries. It will never be sold to chai-sipping professional art collectors in black berets. These writers painted their murals in the most wretched of places, where few will ever see them. And they didn't just scrawl a tag and flee—they did it purposefully, with full intent and commitment. Here in the tunnel, Freedom, Sane, and Smith poured their hearts out to these unseen walls.

As the five of us stand together around the piece, our enthusiasm to escape diminishes. We've hiked through dirt and grime to get here because this isn't something available in the city above. We've followed in the footsteps of the mole people and uncovered the graffiti masters of a phantom metropolis. Josh takes out his camera and begins to shoot.

THREE THE APOTHEOSIS OF CURVES:
CITY HALL SUBWAY

⚠️

Mission	CITY HALL SUBWAY STATION, AUGUST 2001
Location	UNDERNEATH CITY HALL PARK, MANHATTAN
Goal	TO GAIN ACCESS TO THE SHOWPIECE OF THE ORIGINAL IRT SYSTEM OPENED IN 1904, NOW ABANDONED
Officers	LEFTY LEIBOWITZ, L. B. DEYO
Team	SPECIAL AGENT RENÉE, JOSH, MIKE

REPORTED BY ▼

Lefty Leibowitz

Lefty

Down between the walls of shadow
Where the iron laws insist,
   The hunger voices mock.

The worn wayfaring men
With the hunched and humble shoulders,
   Throw their laughter into toil.
                    Carl Sandburg, "Subway"

I'M OUT OF BREATH as I arrive at Jinx headquarters, a cramped office above a Chinese hardware store on Grand Street, an hour past our agreed-to rendezvous time. L.B., Renée, Josh, and Mike have already arrived, punctually as always, and are gathered around the main area. They're gracious in their greeting, but I know from past experience that urban explorers don't like to be kept waiting—especially when the culmination of a long-sought-after discovery is at hand.

The dress and comportment of today's team of explorers rebukes the sensibilities of modern fashion. Their discipline and adherence to the Jinx uniform is complete: The men, as usual, wear dark suits and sunglasses, with hair closely cropped. Renée is well turned out in shades of her own, along with a black knee-length dress. There is not a T-shirt or pair of short pants in sight. The fields of philosophy and science will never take our empirical findings seriously if we dress like adolescents.

Today's mission is to explore the abandoned City Hall subway station, once the crown jewel of the Interborough Rapid Transit (IRT), now a ghostly platform visited only by empty 6 trains during their route-ending U-turns.

The city has protected the station from trespassers and vandals, with the result that even today, fifty-six years after its closing, its arched ceilings and tiled mosaics look much as they did when the station first opened.

The aesthetics of that past have always held a special allure for me. I rarely listen to contemporary music. I don't believe in getting my hair cut by anyone under sixty years old. The stoops of my father's Brooklyn childhood capture my imagination more than the modern skyscrapers of midtown. Our twenty-first-century culture is shoddy and graceless. Our voyage to the station will be a trip back in time to when a subway station was crafted as an aesthetic masterpiece (the City Hall station was designed by the architects of the Cathedral of St. John the Divine). Today we will discover a pinnacle of New York's architectural past hidden from the prying eyes of the slovenly modern citizen.

THE FIRST SUBWAY LINE

The first day of operation for the IRT line, the first subway line in New York City, was October 27, 1904. The opening was the culmination of four years of backbreaking work by a team of over 7,700 laborers who had been assembled to build the 9.1-mile stretch from City Hall to 145th Street in Manhattan. The men, African- and Irish-Americans, along with Italian and German immigrants, risked death and injury daily. Forty-four men lost their lives and thousands more were injured tunneling through thousands of tons of bedrock, all without the benefits of modern machinery or tunneling methods.

The impetus for all of this work was the ever-expanding population of New York City and the attendant transportation needs of its people. At the turn of the nineteenth century, New York had already become one of the most densely populated cities in the world and the point of arrival for the majority of the twenty-four million immigrants who arrived on American shores between 1824 and 1924. In the winter of 1888, a particularly harsh winter storm blanketed the city in an ocean of snow, paralyzing its outdated transportation system of wagons, horses, carriages, and pedestrians. The outcry for an underground train system became deafening. The plan to move forward was approved by 1894, and construction began six years later in 1900.

When the opening night of the IRT finally arrived, the public's excitement had expanded to rival the mood at the opening of any public works project ever completed in New York. Social and civic leaders dressed in formal attire and spent the evening riding the entire length of the line, from one end to the other and back again. They were joined by Mayor George B. McClellan (son of the Civil War general), who symbolically drove the subway's first car prior to the public opening.

The aesthetic high point of the new line was the City Hall subway station, designed by the architectural firm of Heins and LaFarge, who had recently finished designs for the Bronx Zoo and the aforementioned Cathedral of St. John the Divine. This most refined of stations served the public for over thirty-nine years, until it was closed on December 31, 1945. The need for modern stations able to accommodate the increasing lengths of the trains resulted in another sacrifice of beauty to convenience in the modern age. But rumor has it that the station's opulence is preserved even today, and any explorer intrepid enough to gain access will witness what *House & Garden* magazine, in 1904, called the "apotheosis of curves."

WE SET OUT

As we set out for the twenty-minute walk from headquarters to City Hall, I grumpily try to smooth back my tousled and unwashed hair. As co-officer of the expedition, I owe it to the others to be impeccably groomed and turned out like a peacock in full plumage. Today's events have conspired against me, however. My alarm failed to wake me at the appropriate time, and instead of partaking in my complete morning preparations, I was forced to bolt out the door, an hour late, disheveled and ragged, though still dressed in my pinstriped suit and shades. The others kindly pretend not to notice, though I catch L.B. shooting a disapproving glare my way from behind his one-armed sunglasses.

The first few blocks on our excursion are remnants of the old Lower East Side, where Italian and Eastern European immigrants—many Jewish—crowded ten to an apartment at the turn of the nineteenth century and beyond. By the end of the 1960s, most had fled the neighborhood, which had become increasingly beset by poverty, crime, and drugs. Though mostly Hispanic today, signs of the old neighborhood remain along Essex Street, where countless rabbinical supply shops ply their trade. One storefront, selling nothing but accordions, is appropriately named Main Squeeze. Accordions are used in a variety of musical styles, ranging from German and Czech polkas to Mexican *conjunto*, but I wonder if the main customers of this particular shop are the klezmer-playing Orthodox Jews across the river in Williamsburg, Brooklyn.

After crossing Allen Street at Grand, the vestiges of the old Lower East Side pass away instantly and we find ourselves in the heart of Chinatown. The once-small enclave has ravenously expanded, the population estimated by some to be as high as 150,000. This mass of immigrants makes up the largest Chinatown in the United States and also the highest concentration of Chinese in the entire Western Hemisphere. There are few non-Chinese faces among the pressing crowds that mob the fish and vegetable markets, only an odd European tourist with his nose pressed into a tour book. The signage is also entirely Chinese, as are the offerings at the local news kiosks. I glance at the papers for sale at one: no *New York Times,* no *New York Post,* no *Daily News*—only stacks of title after title in Mandarin, Cantonese, and other Chinese languages. We quicken our pace to shorten the time spent inhaling the acrid scent of the fish markets in the August air.

THE CLAY PIGEON OF CHINATOWN

Like the City Hall station that is the object of today's mission, a walk through Chinatown is an open window to the lost history of the city. Its small, curving streets, storefront Buddhist temples, and fortune-tellers are a direct link to the time when the earth beneath this neighborhood was being excavated for the creation of the new IRT: a time when stylish old-world gangsters still roamed the streets.

By 1904, the same year the City Hall subway station was opened to the public, Chinatown was already a thriving immigrant community, with well over 13,000 members. Most had moved to New York City from earlier homes on America's West Coast, where they had worked in railroad construction and gold mining in the mid-nineteenth century. Increased hostility from white workers, including several race riots and harsh discrimination, forced them to larger cities in the East.

Once in New York, they formed close-knit, insular communities, due to both discrimination and self-segregation. Chinatown grew quickly despite such measures as the draconian Chinese Exclusion Act of 1882. The act forbade all Chinese immigration and naturalization until it was repealed in 1943, when it became a liability in the relationship the United States had with Chiang Kai-shek's anti-Japanese forces in World War II.

An interesting feature of Chinatown in 1904 was the sexual imbalance of the population. Because immigration laws forbade wives from joining their husbands in the United States, men outnumbered women by a factor of one hundred to one, a reality that strengthened Chinatown's reputation as a haven of prostitution and opium dens. Stories about young white girls being addicted to opium and enslaved circulated among hysterical citizens.

Various fraternal organizations, or *tongs,* began to spring up to protect the less wealthy Chinese and provide social contacts. Over time, this purportedly benign assistance to new immigrants began to take the form of traditional Mafia-style protection rackets. The gangs were connected to opium, prostitution, and illegal gambling in Chinatown.

The story of the New York tongs begins in 1870, with the arrival of Tom Lee and his On Leong (Peaceful Dragon) Tong. This first tong quickly took control of the illegal activity in Chinatown. Its sophistication and business diversification would later be compared to that of Italy's Cosa Nostra.

Within twenty years, a second tong had been formed. The Hip Sing (Prosperous Union) was at first a relatively insignificant competitor to the On Leong. It wasn't until

1900, when a new tong leader by the name of Mock Duck took over, that it began to challenge the On Leong for power.

Mock Duck quickly began to build his reputation as the "Clay Pigeon of Chinatown," so called because he was able to survive so many assassination attempts. He never ventured outside without two .45s and a hatchet, along with his chain-mail shirt and a bodyguard. If attacked, he would squat down, shut his eyes, and begin firing in both directions.

Mock Duck quickly began to muscle his way into a piece of the On Leong action, and the results were predictably bloody. Brutal tong wars ensued, with the white press reporting on the daily activities of the Chinatown "hatchet men." The battles continued to escalate, including the use of bombs in the 1920s, until U.S. health and immigration officials threatened massive deportations.

Both the On Leong and Hip Sing tongs still operate today on a national scale. They continue their involvement in money laundering, heroin distribution, prostitution, technology theft, and extortion. Their criminal networks include groups such as the Ghost Shadow and Wah Ching gangs, as well as the various Chinese triads.

Luckily, my own experience with the Chinese underworld has been limited to movies and odd anecdotes I've heard over the years. When I was a teenager, I believed that if you walked into any restaurant in Chinatown and signed the check "Flying Dragons" (a tong-affiliated street gang), you could eat for free. I still haven't gotten around to trying that one, but I suspect it would result in an urban adventure of an entirely different sort.

FUNCTION AND FORM

After leaving Chinatown, we move hurriedly through the Civic Center. The streets here are lined with government buildings complete with Roman columns and porticos—a far cry from the low-rise squalor of Chinatown that we've just left behind. As I walk down Centre Street, I am flanked on the left by the city's main courthouses, white stone monuments to justice. These structures do more than put a roof over a jury and a judge: They radiate the authority and prestige of the city and tie its legacy to those of the great democracies of history. Function was not complete without the augmentation of form.

Ahead I see City Hall Park. I ask the others which subway station we are headed to. I know that the abandoned City Hall station lies adjacent to an active platform underneath the actual City Hall building, but I'm unsure which line will provide the closest access point. Renée, who had found some maps of the ghost station on the Internet, informs me that we have to get to the uptown platform of the 6 train at the City Hall/Brooklyn Bridge station. I pause: Should an explorer of my caliber trust an unconfirmed map from the Internet?

Soon we see, directly to the east of City Hall, the stairway leading down to the target station. Josh and Mike have stopped fifty yards back to prepare their camera equipment. The rest of us stop to wait. We watch as Josh and Mike struggle to unload and set up. I worry that the sight of two guys walking around with seventy pounds of photo gear will draw unwanted attention to the team.

Down the stairwell, we enter the city's subway system. Each of us moves through the turnstiles to enter the station proper. It is a typical example of a modern New York subway station—dirty and disheveled, but stripped of the more extreme menace that it held fifteen years ago, when crime, graffiti, panhandling, and homelessness were endemic. It is also far more crowded than we'd hoped. The additional pedestrian traffic will make it harder for us to access the tracks unseen, making an already difficult task now even more challenging. The City Hall subway station is located at the far southern end of Manhattan, at the fringes of the financial district. The majority of commuters who use the station to get to work during the week should be safely ensconced in other parts of the metropolitan area on a Saturday. The crowd we see here today is a combination of fanny-pack-wearing tourists here to see the Brooklyn Bridge and City Hall, and bedraggled travelers switching from the 6 train to the 4 or 5 trains to continue the trip home to Brooklyn. We'll try to blend in, if that's possible for a group of five Jinx agents.

The tracks are a flurry of subway cars thundering by at regular (and brief) intervals. The 6 train, which is local, along with the express 4 and 5 trains arrive and depart the station with alarming speed. With every passing thirty seconds another train races by. The plan is to descend to the tracks and run the fifty or so yards to the old, abandoned part of the station before we encounter any trains. As we stand there, it is easy to doubt the wisdom of our method. I can already envision dodging the oncoming trains as we navigate ourselves down the subway tunnel on foot. It seems like a good recipe for death. I remember, ruefully, the many stories I've read in the New York tabloids of commuters getting pushed in front of oncoming trains by maniacs. The results have rarely been pleasant.

We cluster on the northbound platform while Renée

unfolds her map and examines its rendering of the platform's design. According to her information, the trains loop around on the north side before heading back uptown. The old City Hall station is right next to the loop.

"Wouldn't the trains loop around at the south end in order to head back uptown?" Josh asks. He takes the map and flips it around 180 degrees, so that everything becomes reversed. What was a few seconds ago the north end of the station has now become the south end.

I squint at the map. There is no compass on it, no way to tell which way is up. Nobody is quite sure what to do. This decision is not a trivial one. If we go the wrong way we will be far more likely to have a run-in with a train. The day's exploration would come to a bloody close.

Eventually, we decide that the southbound platform is our best bet. The group heads to the end of the platform, where we hope to descend to the tracks for our journey. When we arrive, we find another obstacle: a fifteen-foot-wide by ten-foot-high steel observation box that houses, on the other side of a pane of thick, clear plastic, an employee of the Metropolitan Transit Authority (MTA). He has a clear vision of the entire platform from where he sits, and a bank of television monitors assists him where his vision is obscured. There is no way that we'll be able to get onto the tracks without being seen.

"Maybe we should come back at night," I say to the group, which is now huddling fifty feet from the MTA monitor. L.B. throws out an alternate approach: What if we take the express tracks? They run parallel to the local tracks, both accessible from the platform on which we stand and less visible to the MTA monitor. It's possible we could jump onto the tracks without being seen.

It's a risky plan. I'm concerned about our large group

crossing over several sets of tracks in heavy train traffic. I look around at the faces of my companions. Most stare ahead silently. I don't know what they are more afraid of—the danger of getting caught or injured, or the prospect of failing to meet our mission goals. Together, the team of L.B., Renée, Josh, and Mike is a hardened veteran crew of explorers. After all the talk of our big plans for C-1609, no one wants the mission to be a disappointment.

"Maybe we can sneak onto an out-of-service Six train and ride past the station?" Renée asks.

It's not a bad idea. We can detour around the rats and third rails, and if the train moves slowly enough we can jump onto the platform and explore on foot. That would ensure a hair-raising return trip, as we'd be forced to find a different method of getting back to civilization. Would we be able to walk back on the tracks? Could we find an exit out to the street from the abandoned station itself? Or would we have to try to leap back onto a passing train? Whatever the case, our prior planning would be of no use to us as we struggled to improvise an escape.

We walk back to the middle of the platform, out of view of the MTA monitor, who is by now eyeing us suspiciously, and wait for the next train to arrive. Thirty seconds later it does, roaring into the station, packed full of straphangers.

"Last stop, Brooklyn Bridge!" the loudspeaker booms. "This train is out of service. Last stop. No passengers."

The doors open, and hundreds of riders pour out through the narrow doorways until the train is empty. Only a young European tourist couple, huddled together uncomprehending, remain. We board the train and grab seats as far from the windows as possible.

"This train is out of service. No passengers."

Renée and L.B. sit close together on the east side of the train while Josh and Mike sit directly across from them. I'm about fifteen feet down, alone. The European couple, both wearing neon shorts and sneakers, are another fifteen feet away. They sit there staring, confused at the sudden influx of dark-suited, sunglass-wearing newcomers.

Then the doors close. The train isn't moving.

The conductor must be walking through each car now, making sure that there's no one on the train, I think to myself. It's just a matter of time before we're back to square one. The last thing I need is another trespassing charge, or worse, a fine. My money is earmarked for the purchase of a beautiful white silk suit, like the one Ric Flair used to wear back in his NWA championship days. I don't have any chump change lying around to buy off Johnny Law.

Ten more seconds pass. Suddenly the train lurches forward. We're moving. Smiles break out on the faces of my fellow explorers. The Europeans look even more nervous. What could we be so damn happy about?

The train is moving along at moderate speed now, through the darkened tunnel at the end of the line. I look out the window, straining to see any signs of the abandoned City Hall station. Is it possible we're going the wrong way? Or that we got on the wrong train?

In the next moment, the twilight of the tunnel brightens. We're not on the wrong train. We enter the long anticipated ghost station. It's not well lit, and it's obvious that the years of disuse have taken a toll in rust and water damage, but it's clear that what's buried underneath the layers of grime is unlike the stations I'm used to.

THE TOMB STATION

As the train moves through the station, I press my face to the glass and strain to see as much detail as possible. The first feature I notice is the elaborate system of mosaics and tiles that decorate the walls. Heins and LaFarge had wanted the station to be decorated with a series of garlands, wreaths, scrolls, and rosettes, so they hired several firms to help them with this task. The result is an ornate cluster of terra cotta and ceramic shining with bright colors from one end of the tunnel to the other. It's an urban version of King Tut's tomb, with the five Jinx agents playing the role of Lord Carnarvon in 1923.

The architects also commissioned the Guastavino Construction Company to create a series of structural arches and vaulted ceilings. Skylights made from amethyst glass allowed natural light to filter in and illuminate the station. I've read that the light was once augmented by a series of brass chandeliers, though as we pass through the station I see no sign of them.

This station is different from those used on a daily basis around the city. Those stations provide a tunnel for the train and a turnstile for my tokens or MetroCard. They are passably clean. There are a few benches to sit on. Beyond these efficiencies, however, their creators seem to have made little effort to create an environment that delights the senses. This station, on the other hand, is gorgeous. Just looking out the window onto its sumptuous platform, I can feel the romance of the past.

The train is stopped now, apparently waiting for a signal change before continuing the loop to the uptown track. All of us, the European tourists now included, stare out the windows. Josh and Mike are furiously snapping picture after picture through the thick plastic of the train window.

Suddenly, someone remembers that this is our best chance to disembark from the train and to get into the station on foot. Josh, Mike, and L.B. rush to the door that connects the cars and step out onto the small area between trains. I stay where I am. I've read the signs that warn not to ride between cars and the articles about teenagers who've fallen to their deaths trying to jump off. Plus someone needs to keep an eye on Renée and the Europeans and make sure they stay out of harm's way. Who would protect them if I were to get injured jumping onto the platform?

I stand on the train and listen to the commotion coming from between the trains. It is not more than three seconds before the train lurches into motion once more.

"Are you guys still there?" I shout out to L.B., Josh, and Mike. I have no idea if they are on the train, on the platform, or in the process of being ground up into tiny bits beneath the steel wheels of the subway.

They file back into the car one by one and sit down. There were no injuries, but the train was not stopped long enough for them to disembark.

Soon we are out of the station and back in the darkened subway tunnel. Another thirty seconds and the doors open up on the northbound platform. The five of us, along with our European fellow travelers, step gingerly out from the train and back to the hustle-bustle world of the New York commuter.

The expedition has barely been a success. Although we got to see something that very few people will ever see, we haven't explored the ghost station on foot. The other explorers wear a wide range of expressions. Josh seems relieved that we've avoided walking on the tracks. Renée and Mike are hard to read—they seem content with having caught a glimpse of the station. L.B. looks sullen and distraught. I remember seeing the same expression on his face toward the end of the Croton Aqueduct mission, when we finally turned around after having our path blocked by ever-deepening water. He tells me later that he felt as if the station was taunting him from behind the glass windows of the subway car that carried us. He is the Jinx Project's very own Tantalus, who thirsted and starved in Hades, unable to eat or drink though surrounded by fruit and water.

I can understand the feeling of disappointment, but as explorers, we also have to take measure of the inherent risks of a given situation and make our judgments accordingly. No one has ever gotten injured on any of our explorations. We don't consider ourselves to be reckless daredevils. We push as far as we can, but when things get too dangerous, we know when to stop. We've got a lot more expeditions yet to come.

A TUNNEL THROUGH TIME

As I stand on the Brooklyn Bridge station platform in my soot-stained suit, the active station looks nothing like the opulent ghost station we've just glimpsed. The design is austere and basic, the principal design objective being efficiency, not allure. In the popular imagination, the past was a time when the beautiful and the useful blended together seamlessly. Our trip back in time today is further evidence to support this popular prejudice.

The Jinx aesthetic allows us to pay homage to this idea. In his daily life and on his explorations, in his dress and in his work, the Jinx agent stands as a paragon of class and elegance. He is a bulwark against the forces of incivility and sloth, just as Columbus and De Gama stood for progress and science. His urban exploration must be twofold in its ambition: to discover the unknown amidst the bored and apathetic and to promote the sublime amidst the crass and vulgar. He is unfailingly modest, yet never forgets that the fates of nations hinge on his every act.

All around us lay the ruins of a golden age of style: the graceful curve of a decaying underground arch, the fading fedora on the elderly man's head, the monstrous gargoyles overlooking the city from twenty stories up. Mostly we don't notice. But just as an archaeologist digs beneath the surface to uncover layers of meaning and clues to the past, so does the urban explorer enter into a dialogue with the living ruins of the city. Despite the constant building and development in the modern, vibrant metropolis, the old world lives on.

FOUR

THE GOD'S-EYE VIEW:

GRAND CENTRAL TERMINAL

Attach label, or print or type

Mission
GRAND CENTRAL TERMINAL, JUNE 2001

Location
MIDTOWN MANHATTAN

Goal
TO FIND EVIDENCE OF FDR'S SECRET TUNNEL FROM
THE TRAIN TUNNELS TO THE WALDORF-ASTORIA; TO
GAIN ACCESS TO THE ROOF OF THE WALDORF-ASTORIA

Officers
LEFTY LEIBOWITZ, L. B. DEYO

Team
SPECIAL AGENT RENÉE, BRAD WIENERS, KIKÉ ARENAL,
JOSH, STEVE DUNCAN, AND BRAZEN

REPORTED BY ▼

Lefty Leibowitz

Lefty

Wealth I ask not, hope nor love,
Nor a friend to know me;
All I ask, the heaven above
And the road below me.

Robert Louis Stevenson,
"The Vagabond"

GRAND CENTRAL TERMINAL, New York's iconic landmark, is also the scene of the Jinx Project's greatest humiliation. In 1987, at the age of sixteen, L.B. and I, along with a third friend, accessed its roof and leapt across its ledges and machinery until a phalanx of angry police officers stormed the roof and arrested us. We were escorted to the terminal's police station and held for the next six hours, where our clothes and bags were scoured in endless searches. Rotating shifts of officers subjected us to games of "good cop/bad cop." One policeman argued for leniency; the other suggested that we be sent to Rikers Island and "made brides of."

To this day, it's the only time that we've ever gotten into trouble with the law. We've never forgotten the indignation that we suffered.

So like any fools who don't know when they're beat, we're going back to Grand Central Station. We're going to infiltrate its underground of soot and grime, and eventually make our way back to its roof. And this time we won't get caught.

Every day five hundred thousand commuters use this depot, its beehive pace a fitting welcome to New York. The concourse floor, a half-acre of polished white

Tennessee marble, shines with the lights that cascade down from the ceiling and illuminate the entire waiting area with a cathedral-like glow.

The windows stretch up 125 feet to the ceiling, dwarfing the commuters. Though the station's opulent exterior and Beaux Arts architecture are the stuff of Hollywood, very few know about the inner workings of the terminal: the machinery that generates its power, the tunnels that house the tracks, the vital organs of its underbelly.

Memories of our arrest lie heavily on my mind as I gather with the rest of the team in Grand Central's main waiting room. Present are L.B., Renée, Brad Wieners, Kiké, Josh, Steve Duncan, and Brazen.

For years I've heard stories about the tunnels underneath Grand Central. Some say there is a secret passageway that leads directly from the tunnels to the Waldorf-Astoria Hotel on 49th Street, used by Franklin Roosevelt during his administration for direct access. According to my research, a power station for Grand Central occupied part of the modern Waldorf-Astoria site, and a loading dock underneath the power station was never destroyed when the hotel was built. Even though it was not built specifically for the hotel, someone realized that it might make an ideal departure point for guests who needed to avoid the crowds at the terminal.

A *New York Times* article from September 8, 1929, titled "New Waldorf Gets Own Rail Siding," reads:

The new Waldorf-Astoria Hotel, to be erected in the block bounded by Park Avenue, Lexington Avenue, Forty-ninth and Fiftieth Streets, will have a private railway siding underneath the building, it was learned yesterday. Guests with private rail cars may have them routed directly to the hotel instead of to the Pennsylvania Station or the Grand Central Terminal, and may leave their cars at a special elevator which will take them directly to their suites or to the lobby.

The arrangement is made possible because of the fact that the New York Central tracks pass directly beneath the block, which has been obtained by the Hotel Waldorf-Astoria Corporation from the New York Central Railroad "air rights" on the site.

According to noted subway historian Joseph Brennan, an elevator and stairway lead up to an adjacent doorway alongside the hotel's entrance on 49th Street, but never led to the hotel interior proper. An additional staircase on the other end of the secret platform leads up to 50th Street. FDR is rumored to have used the former after delivering a foreign policy speech on October 24, 1944. There are also whispers of the platform having been used by General John J. Pershing in 1938 and for a party thrown by Andy Warhol in 1965.

Regardless, there's only one way to find out for sure. We start off our expedition by moving down to the lower level of the concourse, where we will gain access to the labyrinthine tunnels below. The upper concourse is still busy, even at ten o'clock at night, with commuters on their way back home to New York's northern suburbs. The lower concourse is far quieter, and I hope the inactivity will help us access the tunnels undetected.

But as we begin to move through the lower concourse and scope out the track entrances, I notice an impressive police presence in the station. There are at least six cops actively patrolling the lower level, and the sight of them puts my nerves on edge. If a cop should see us go through a door to an out-of-service track, suspicion would be aroused. The mission would have to be aborted, or we'd face certain incarceration.

We gather in a small alcove near the escalator and peer out at the series of doors that lead to the tracks. Are they locked? Which one should we try? Are the cops watching us now?

"Let's go through this door," L.B. whispers as he gestures toward one of the track entrances. "One at a time. Make sure to wait until the person ahead of you is completely through the door. If anyone is looking at you, don't go through. Wait until the coast is clear."

Renée moves through the door first, while the rest of us wait fifty feet away around a corner that leads to the food court, which is closed this time of night. As she disappears behind the door, we stand perfectly still, anxious to see if she will be ejected. Thirty seconds pass without incident, and we suppose she has entered safely. Either that, or she's been whisked away in handcuffs. Have we overlooked some flaw in our plan?

Nevertheless, L.B. purposefully strides toward the entranceway and also disappears into the passage. More time passes, and more silence.

Each explorer now follows in turn: Brazen, mind racing at the prospect of delving fifteen levels into the earth; Brad, the fearless man-giant of *Outside* magazine; Kiké and Josh, cameras at the ready; Steve Duncan, the adrenaline-addled youth with the punk rock style; and finally, me, the brave Caudillo of the Project. I slip through the doorway only after making sure that no one has been left behind.

We stand on an abandoned train platform that during rush hour holds hundreds of people. It is completely deserted now, though still as well lit as at peak times. The desolation of the depopulated platform clashes with its cheerful brightness. Quickly, we move to the end of the platform in a group.

As we march closer to the end, the platform begins to narrow and darken. We are now one hundred yards away from our initial access point, and the pillars that support the ceiling of this tunnel cast long shadows across the floor. Suddenly, with only a quick look in both directions, L.B. jumps down onto the tracks and scurries up to an adjacent platform, using a covered third rail as a step.

Josh shouts out, "Are these third rails live?"

"Probably so," L.B. responds, "but as long as you don't touch the rail itself you should be okay. They're all covered, you know."

The team is delighted to know that they *should* be okay and that the rails are only *probably* live.

I move down onto the tracks and search for a means to climb up to the next platform. There's no way off the track without using the third rail as a stepladder. With fingers crossed and a prayer on my lips, I carefully place my foot on the rail covering and push myself onto the platform. I brace for the jolt of deadly current, but feel nothing. The rail covering, with a little help from my twenty-dollar Payless shoes, has insulated me well.

Encouraged by my non-electrocution, the rest of the team follows. An ominous-looking open doorway leading to a darkened descending staircase sits fifteen feet ahead of us and to the right, in the wall of the easternmost platform.

Again, L.B. enters the doorway first, followed by each of the team members. We move down the metal staircase into an industrial hell. Huge pipes, two feet in diameter, line each wall of this new corridor, and puddles of stagnant water lie on the unfinished concrete floor. The pipes intermittently shoot out scorching blasts of steam. One blast comes within inches of hitting Brazen's face as he moves down the staircase. He seems not to notice.

I see Kiké smirk as he watches the scene from a few feet away. As *Outside* magazine's ace photographer, Kiké risks injury and death shooting war zones and natural disasters. He's not impressed by would-be secret agents crawling around in a train tunnel. We're not exactly confronting the Shining Path in the Amazon, after all.

Slowly, we move down the corridor. The heat from the steam pipes is unbearable, and sweat coats our faces. Renée shrugs off the unpleasant conditions and pushes to the head of the pack.

Thoughts of the tunnel's construction run through my mind. Visions of broken men, covered in soot and grime, paint an ugly portrait of life at the turn of the century.

THE BEGINNINGS OF THE TERMINAL

The original Grand Central Depot, a terminal for steam locomotives, had been opened in October 1871 under the sponsorship of shipping magnate Cornelius Vanderbilt. It was obsolete almost immediately and the following thirty years saw a series of expansions and renovations. In 1902, a horrible collision in the Park Avenue Tunnel took the lives of seventeen people, and there was an outcry for an answer to safety, noise, and pollution problems. The natural solution was to move to electric trains.

A plan was hatched to convert the station to electricity, and a massive effort was soon under way. Workers toiled for ten years to excavate 2.8 million pounds of earth and rock for the new tunnels. The railyard's grade was lowered to an average of thirty feet below street level.

All in all, the construction cost $80 million (roughly $2 billion in today's money). The costs were partly defrayed by paving over the area immediately to the north of the station, which had previously been used as an open-air railyard for the steam locomotives. The newly paved areas were leased to developers and soon landmark buildings like the Waldorf-Astoria began to sprout up to join Grand Central Terminal in its mythic urban status.

At the same time, work was going on to complete the design and construction of the aboveground portion of the terminal. The result of that labor is a train station unrivaled in scale and beauty. The exterior façade as you face north toward 42nd Street on Park Avenue is renowned for its fifty-foot-high pediment featuring gargantuan statues of the Roman gods Mercury, Minerva, and Hercules astride a thirteen-foot clock. The main concourse, which can handle five hundred thousand commuters a day, could almost fit a city block. It's 120 feet wide, 375 feet long, and 125 feet high. Five gold chandeliers were put in place in the terminal, each containing a staggering 144 lightbulbs. A map of the constellations was painted on the 125-foot-high ceiling of the main concourse. It features 2,500 stars, though they were painted on backward, giving commuters a God's eye view of the heavens.

This display of opulence and splendor has had to fend off several developer attempts to level the terminal, as had happened with New York's original Pennsylvania Station. Because of the work of preservationists (most famously Jacqueline Kennedy in the early 1970s), Grand Central still stands today, a monument to the craftsmanship of a bygone era.

THE UNDERGROUND AWAITS

The history of the terminal and the workers who perspired here day after day are the ghosts that follow us today. So much of the endeavor of building a Grand Central Terminal occurred behind the scenes, out of the view of the millions who ride the trains and stroll through the public archways of the waiting room.

Josh takes out his camera and snaps away at every pipe and puddle in this twisted and convoluted maze of machinery. Kiké matches him shot for shot.

Steve Duncan walks in the rear, closely examining the rough exteriors and fittings on the pipes. They seem to be carrying steam, but to what end? Like most of the explorers on today's mission, Duncan is entering the underbelly of Grand Central for the first time. A few yards ahead a staircase leads back up to the tracks. We will need to follow them if we are to find the passage to the Waldorf. We'll need to risk being flattened by the trains roaring by at full acceleration and to avoid the fatigued glances of their cargo of drowsy commuters. I remember Julia from Dark Passage's first attempt to follow the tracks to their destination; she was caught by a station employee and forced to leave. Her feminine charm enabled her to escape, but it might not be so easy for us. The terminal's maintenance workers patrol the tracks in great numbers. The chances of being spotted are high.

At the top of the stairs we find ourselves on the same tracks we left a short while ago, only now we are several hundred yards to the north and the platforms are no longer in view. Brad Wieners picks up a discarded yellow hard hat and places it on his head. The tracks crisscross each other in dizzying knots. The air is still warm, but the absence of the steam pipes has lowered the temperature back to a reasonable zone. The walls and ground are black with soot and dirt, and train tunnel debris—railroad spikes, papers, construction vests—is littered all around. The walls are raw here—rough and unfinished, as if the tunnel were blasted in a great hurry. There is no detailing or attention to aesthetics. This tunnel was not meant to be beautiful.

We walk north along the tracks, continuing to head away from the terminal. I'm unsure whether we are moving toward the alleged passageway to the Waldorf, but I'm hoping that if we stay the course we will stumble upon some clue. Steve Duncan maneuvers gracefully around obstacles and third rails, the joy at being among the trains apparent on his face. The telltale rumbling of a commuter train can be heard in the distance.

We scramble to find a place to hide. The glowing headlight of a Metro-North train shines in the distance, and the screeching of steel grows ever louder. The train whips by at breakneck speed, wind pouring off its surface and blasting our faces. After the train has passed only the eerie, echoing silence of the tunnel remains.

Another hundred yards up we see a decrepit, five-rung ladder propped up against the western wall of the tunnel. It leads up to the entranceway of a small alcove built into the side of the rock. It's shrouded in darkness and covered in oily grime. L.B. ascends the ladder.

"Check this out," he shouts. "It looks like someone has been living here." I follow him up into the alcove and discover a homemade bridge inside: a wooden door across a gap in the concrete floor. I tentatively place my weight on the makeshift bridge. The door creaks with the burden, but holds.

"You guys should come up here. There's stuff here to

shoot," L.B. yells down to Kiké and Josh. Kiké climbs into the alcove, while Josh shoots from the outside. It's filthy. The rock formations on the walls are coated in black muck, and Kiké has become covered in the damp, sticky residue. Rotting blankets are strewn about.

As L.B. and Kiké burrow further into the darkened cranny, I notice two dark figures in the distance. "Shut up, everyone," I whisper, but it is too late. Flashlight beams shoot across our faces and the shouts of the distant figures echo through the tunnel.

The figures move toward us, and for a moment we freeze in fear. Eyes glance in every direction until suddenly, as if moved by a hidden force, we break into a run at once. We gallop north at full sprint, feet pounding against the ground, our heads pounding with fear of capture. But the figures behind us recede into the distance. Why aren't they following?

Regardless, we know we've been spotted now: It's only a matter of time before we're booted out of here. I can practically hear the radio calls going out to the police officers who patrol the grand concourse. We have to head to the surface.

L.B. spots a staircase leading up from an abandoned platform and wordlessly takes it; the rest of us follow. We climb two flights through absolute darkness, and at the top we reach a closed iron door. The door is unadorned, save for a simple white sign reading, Emergency Exit Only—Alarm Will Sound.

Brazen rests his hand softly on the door, and looks at us for approval. We'll have to make sure we all go through the door at once, so it will be open for the shortest time possible. That way there will be a lesser chance of further alerting the authorities.

Brazen slowly pushes open the door, and the coolness of the outside air hits us in the face. He exits silently, and we follow. Quickly, we turn toward the corner, where we discover that we are at the intersection of 50th and Park. A sign on an adjacent wall says, "Welcome to the Waldorf Hotel."

REGROUPING

Outside, we take a few moments to catch our breath. I look around at the rest of the group, mostly covered in soot and filth. All are exhausted. Have we inadvertently discovered the route that FDR used to travel from the Waldorf to his personal train? The descriptions I've read disagree on whether the secret tunnel runs directly to the hotel or the street directly adjacent to its entrance. But we are also on 50th Street, and, according to Joseph Brennan, the exit leading out to 49th Street is the one that FDR used. It seems as if we've missed tracing his path by one block.

At any rate, it's time for part two of tonight's expedition: the roof of Grand Central Terminal, the resting spot of the mighty Minerva, Mercury, and Hercules. It's been fourteen years since the day L.B. and I were arrested and the ghosts of our past failure await exorcism once and for all.

We head back down Park Avenue and reenter the terminal. Up the staircase near the open unmarked bar that comforts weary commuters, we turn left. Past a huge marble staircase we enter the elevator that serves the administrative offices for the Metro-North commuter line. Above the offices is the roof.

As we approach the top floor on the elevator, a bell rings. The elevator stops and the doors open. A custodial worker stands on the other side of the doors in a drab olive jumpsuit, staring. We stare back.

"Going up?" Josh inquires and then smiles wide, the whites of his teeth glinting from the overhead light. I've been with him in these situations before. The looming specter of authority always brings out the smooth talker in Josh.

My heart speeds noticeably as the worker continues to stare. We must be a sight to see. Eight explorers, all dressed for action and covered in filth, riding a cramped elevator up through a closed office building.

"I'll wait for the next one." The custodian smiles back, and a moment later the doors close. I exhale in relief.

At last on the top floor, we file out of the elevator into a plush office waiting room, fully furnished with couches, greenery, and, most ominously, security cameras. L.B. leads the way and we turn a corner where we find a stairway leading up. We climb the stairs and come to a doorway leading into a maintenance room, filled with mysterious machinery of uncertain utility. Are these the boilers for the terminal? The air is thick with steam and the smell of mildew. I spot a final door across the room. It is open, and I can see the night sky poking in through the doorway. We make our way over, and then through it.

THE ROOF

The roof of Grand Central Terminal is just as I remember it. A half-dozen huge air-conditioning units, each almost two stories high, stand amidst catwalks that weave across its entire expanse. The catwalks snake through every portion of the roof, allowing easy access for maintenance workers. Other unrecognizable industrial machines fill the gaps. All of the monumental skyscrapers of midtown stare down at us from their nearby perches: the looming, blank façade of the MetLife building as well as the Art Deco dazzle of the Chrysler Building.

I scramble over to a nearby air-conditioning unit that stands two stories high. A metal-frame ladder enclosed in a safety cage is bolted to its side, which I carefully scale. From the top of the unit, the view is even better. Below me, the other explorers walk around the roof, most experiencing it for the first time. Immediately to my south I can see the enormous profiles of the gods that stare down onto 42nd Street from the terminal's roof. To my north, Renée and Josh are moving over to the central section of the roof, where an explorer can stand 125 feet above the grand concourse and look down through a hole onto the people below. The roof is sloped here, and they clamber along on the rain-slicked surface, slipping and sliding as they go.

Meanwhile, L.B. and Brad Wieners are climbing another ladder to the outermost portion of the terminal roof, which is even more sloped than the central section. They inch forward cautiously on their way to the great statues. It was here that we were caught in 1987. We had come in broad daylight, during a weekday, oblivious to the fact that bemused office workers surrounded us on all sides. It didn't take long for someone to call the cops.

Back in those days, I had traipsed across this roof with total fearlessness and abandon. Now, I am more cautious. Just being up here scares me, and I worry about my safety. My breath has shortened noticeably and I feel the grime of perspiration and dirt on my face. I want to get back down to ground level. The potential for death and disfigurement lies around every corner. Perhaps this consciousness of mortality, this awakening of fear, is one of the things that separates urban exploration from our teenage high jinks of 1987. Now we don't just want thrills and risk, we want to discover, to find something new. The adrenaline rush is still important, but ultimately it is the element of discovery that makes urban exploration different from, say, bungee jumping. I think that other veteran explorers, like the fifty-year-old men in San Francisco who routinely plan climbs of the Golden Gate Bridge, would agree.

I look once more at the statue of Mercury, the god of speed and skill and the patron of travelers, and see the black and yellow of the Jinx flag flapping in the wind alongside the god's staff, the caduceus. L.B. has somehow made it up onto the god's stone wing and marked this roof as Jinx territory. It is an exclamation of our redemption, and a new beginning for C-1609.

"The only *what* around?" he shrieks. "Not *restaurant*. The place isn't fit for criminals!"

"Stop that, will you? What are you doing?" I hiss, lowering my outstretched hand to push down the volume. "Those construction trailers still have lights on. There could be people—"

"They'll never get us all," Nick says.

Brain defies me, pitching his voice higher. "I'm *poisoned*!" he moans. "God help me. It was the *beef*!" He stops dead in his tracks and lifts his plaintive eyes to heaven.

"You're not *poisoned*, Brain—"

"*Not poisoned?*" He coils as if to strike, then sags under the weight of his infirmity. "How can *you* know? Have you ever eaten anything that wasn't—Christ, I'm talking to an Irishman about *food*! Listen, my insides can't handle McDonald's. I'm not accustomed to eating *garbage* from a pig's *trough*!"

I have to stop my hand from clamping his mouth shut. The nearest trailer is just a few yards away. Pedestrians are strolling just outside the fence. "Okay," I say. "Renée has some Alka-Seltzer in her bag, I think. You should—"

"Alka Seltzer!" Brain snarls. "The fourth course in the *American meal*!"

"Brain, it'll straighten you right out."

Brain plants his feet and juts his chin out. "You couldn't get me to—*Alka*-Seltzer? Are you crazy?" His voice, lower now, retains its menace. "If you had *ten men* holding me down you couldn't force Alka-Seltzer down my throat. Christ, talk about poisoning—you think I'm going to swallow some weird *mineral*? And nobody really even knows *what* the stuff does to your insides—"

THE SURFACE OF NEW YORK, in the summer of 2001, is a thriving human locus to rival any in history. The city encompasses 3.5 million tourists and commuters and 8 million residents on an average weekday, for a population density of 8,000 persons per square mile. The typical New Yorker, if he is a man, is among the most potent in America (sperm count 131.5 million). If a woman, she is among the most beautiful and sophisticated.

The city displays unprecedented highs and lows. It is the financial capital of the world, home of the planet's two largest stock markets. Still, some 30 percent of New Yorkers remain below the poverty line.

Art is dead. Conceptual art functions as editorial cartoon, lacking only punch-line captions. In architecture, postmodern attempts to retreat from austere modernism have been busier, but no less ugly, than their monolithic forebears. Confusion and inexpert fabrication are equally evident in the fashion industry. In 1950, the meanest laborer would scarcely consider leaving home without a jacket, tie, and hat. Today, attorneys and businessmen slouch into their high-rent offices dressed for the beach.

PURGATORY:
THE HIVE
PART II

FIVE INTO THE BREACH:
SMALLPOX HOSPITAL

Attach label, or print or type

Mission	SMALLPOX HOSPITAL, EARLY SUMMER 2001
Location	ROOSEVELT ISLAND
Goal	ENTER, EXPLORE
Officers	LEFTY LEIBOWITZ, L. B. DEYO
Team	STEVE DUNCAN, NICK SCIENCE, BRAZEN, SPECIAL AGENT RENÉE, GABRIEL, BRAIN, JOSH
Observers	BRAD WIENERS, KIKÉ ARENAL (*OUTSIDE* MAGAZINE)

REPORTED BY

L. B. Deyo

L. B. Deyo

What are the roots that clutch, what branches grow
Out of this stony rubbish?

T. S. Eliot, *The Waste Land*

A FURIOUS CROSSWIND rakes the low ground, churning the tall grass. The sky broils red across the skyline. Rain's coming, but not yet. We're inside the fence, past the lunar scars of the construction site, rounding the bend by the southwestern shore of Roosevelt Island, headed for the tree line that conceals the target. We move in loose formation. Steve Duncan is in front, rocking the Kool Moe Dee terminators, almost breaking stride. Close behind him marches Lefty Leibowitz in his shirtsleeves, sweating off the flu, joking with the Arch-Agent Gabriel. Josh hauls thirty pounds of camera equipment and roasts in his black suit, loving every second, and behind him Renée gracefully negotiates the black uneven ground, her hair braided down her back, sunglasses on. *Outside* magazine has sent along the Brobdingnagian Brad Wieners, six foot six and sunburned, blond ponytail, face scarred by adventure, and Kiké Arenal, his Venezuelan photographer, who ten days from now will be chasing down guerrillas in the Colombian jungle. Brazen hustles silently behind them, his face, as always, set in an impassive half-smile. Nick Science tries to raise headquarters on the handheld as I argue with Brain.

"The *McDonald's!*" Brain clutches at his midsection. He's dazed, unshaven, his shades missing. He winces at the ground.

"It was the only thing around," I say. "You should—"

"There it is." Steve Duncan interrupts with a shout from the front of the pack. Turning the corner first, he sees the hospital rearing up against the sky. "Smallpox Hospital," Steve says, "one hundred and fifty years later."

So it is, unwrapped before us like a candy. Smallpox Hospital, the only official New York landmark in ruins, the city's best example of Gothic Revival, the crown jewel of Roosevelt Island. Its face glows in the floodlights, lit up for the commuters on the FDR Drive. Steel beams prop up the masonry. The whiteness of the façade sets off empty windows; it looks like a face with the eyes torn out, an empty skull.

"Stay out of the light," I say. "We can enter from the back."

Everybody picks up the pace now, charging through the damp grass, holding to shadows. The hospital is immense. Already we can see how wild the ruins have become, how densely overgrown. Trees rise sixty and seventy feet up from the rubble of the basement. Nine agents in uniform, with Brad and Kiké close at hand, swing around to the unlit lawn at the Queens side. We head inside the building.

There's not much of an "inside" left to the hospital. A full acre of roof and most of the upper floors are gone. As we enter the ruins, we see Manhattan through the hospital's heavy-lidded eyes, church windows full of light and inspiration. Halogen rays stream through a neglected scaffolding that reaches up five stories into the spires. Everybody's shooting now. Josh and Kiké's shutters chatter, their flashbulbs strobe the brick walls. Renée snaps an empty doorway forty feet above her, nothing on either side of it but treetops.

"Careful," says Renée. She holds the hem of her black dress now, peering intensely at the shifting bricks beneath her feet as we cross through an archway into what had been an adjacent room. The rubble piles up against the wall in a small hill. Half-buried doorways lead down into darkness. At the far side of the room, at the top of the pile, a wooden beam leads down from the second story. Duncan, still at point, reaches the beam first and effortlessly spirits himself up. Now on the second floor, he can peer down to survey the scene. In the closing decades of the nineteenth century, one of every hundred New York deaths happened here, in this broken fortress. Tonight, the flora strangle one another for every inch of earth. The trees spread up and out, attacking the walls as they once destroyed the roof. The greenery whips in the rising wind, flashing electric in the floodlights.

"See how the leaves are upturned?" Renée points for me. "That's the storm coming."

THE STAIRCASE

Duncan can't hear her. He's already inching up the shattered remains of a staircase. The first flight of stairs hangs from the wall in pieces, loose and gapped as a prizefighter's teeth. He grips the metal casements that bolt the stairs to the wall and splays himself like a spider to keep his weight off the steps. He moves quickly and automatically. The basement below him is a void; he can't even tell how far down it goes. Reaching the first landing, he sees he's only past the easy part. The next flight has no steps at all; only a wood plank connects his landing to the next one up.

"Jesus, are those stairs?" Brain asks, now inside.

"They used to be," I say. Then I shout up to Duncan, "Be very careful. At the first sign of collapse, I want to hear you say your prayers."

Duncan doesn't bother to look. He's on the second landing now, settling against it, testing its strength. Still no way to tell how high up he is: at least thirty feet, and the landing has no supports at all.

"That way," I continue, "I'll know you've gone to your reward with a clear conscience."

"And we'll be able to get out from underneath you," says the Brain.

Behind us, Gabriel has entered a side chamber with Lefty and Josh. "This is the autopsy room," he guesses. The floor and walls are tiled, and faucets stab out at unnatural angles. The clinical purpose still shows through fifty years of dust and graffiti. You can see the ghosts of doctors scrubbing up here, sterilizing their instruments. But the illusion ends at the fourth wall or, rather, the yawning hole where the fourth wall once stood. Josh strides to the edge of the floor, letting his gaze drop into yet another basement. The trees and shrubs grow thick down there. Josh says it looks like a jungle.

"It's like Maurice Sendak," says Gabriel. *Where the Wild Things Are.* He pronounces the title respectfully, and we nod in agreement. The ruins recall the dreamscape of the children's story, where the boy's bedroom changes in the darkness. His carpet turns to grass, his closet becomes the mouth of a cave, and wild palms lilt in the starlight.

Brain stands behind them, looking over their shoulders, none the worse for wear. I congratulate him on surviving his Big Mac.

Brain's our own Falstaff: "Wherein cunning but in craft, wherein crafty but in villainy." He lights a cigarette and scowls at me. "Listen, I have a very delicate stomach," he says. "What about you? What's your excuse?"

Excuse for what, I ask him.

"*Ah,* you looked depressed at dinner!" he says. "You didn't even talk to Renée! I thought maybe you'd missed your *Prozac!*"

I tell him I'm fine. "Those customers in the McDonald's got on my nerves."

Brain hadn't noticed the people in the McDonald's. All he remembers is that *special sauce*—

"Just some Lower East Side clowns," I say. "Hipsters, you know. Pretty boys."

Brain's gaze drifts back into the trees as he nods and inhales a Pall Mall.

"Same type as we got taking over the whole city," I say. "Featherweights. Fashion guys. Curly-haired kids. The same downtown punks who been moving in since I got my apartment."

Brain stands silent, his eyes glazing over in the darkness. Is he still with me? He's just staring down into the jungle. Then he says, "Yeah?"

"Yeah. Well, you *asked.*" I hate it when Brain asks a question and then fades out during my answer. Been doing it since we were in grade school. "I shouldn't let them get to me, right? I shouldn't rent them space in my head, I know. But they *ruin everything.* I mean, what are we doing here? We're here because this is a magnificent city, a city in stately decline. When I walk down the street, I want to enjoy the aesthetic. I want to feel the history. And how *can* I? The romance of the experience, you see, is spoiled because on every corner stands some lily-white swain with his lush, flowing locks and his semi-tinted '70s cop shades. It spoils it, because what's the point of being here if it's all just mall rats and club kids? Do you see what I mean? This was the city of Fitzgerald, E. B. White, Cab Calloway, Run-DMC, the Ramones, Dutch Schultz, Meyer Lansky, Alexander Hamilton, Aaron *Burr,* for God's sake. This was Damon Runyon's city! This was Babe Ruth's city. And now these *waifs* are inheriting it!"

"You're obsessed, Laughing Boy."

"Well, God *damn it!*" I implore him. "It's different where you live. In Astoria you've got families of *immigrants,* proud people, hardworking people. Manhattan kids are straight out of a music video. I mean, they rock their faded Smiths T-shirts and cutoff shorts. They go to the same beauty parlors as their girlfriends and walk out with Gabe Kaplan afros. And you think I'm crazy, but they all cultivate this kind of *socialist mystique,* carrying a copy of *Manufacturing Consent* in one hand and an iced coffee in the other, talking on a cell phone. Most of them are petty *traitors.* Sure, you say. But has it occurred to you that these people are a kind of vampire? See, I think that's why they all look so pale and weak. They come to New York and sink their fangs, and they bleed everything white. To walk through the Lower East Side these days, really, *you could almost be in L.A.*"

Brain laughs. "Laughing Boy, do you want to know the real reason you do this urban exploration?"

Preaching has worn me out; I have to catch my breath. "Yeah, what's that?"

"You love buildings," he says, "and you hate people."

CHALLENGE

> "My adventures with Jinx have me convinced that its members could use a few days in the climbing gym—they are clumsy at best. . . ."
>
> **Brad Wieners, "Wild in the Streets,"**
> *Outside* **magazine**

"Hey there." Steve startles us by sticking his head down through a hole in the ceiling. "I think I've found a way to the roof. There's reinforced concrete all the way over—"

"Reinforced!" Brain shouts. "That's a relative term!"

"—it goes all the way over to the other wing, and then stops. I'm going to check it out." His head disappears into the ceiling.

"Stay close to the wall," I call after him. "The floor's weakest near the center, I think."

We turn back into the hallway, where the stairwell dares us to climb. Brazen has been rooting around below, and now catches up with us. "How did he get up there?"

"Took the stairs," I say.

"Those stairs?"

Nick Science jumps in at the dramatic pause to ask a worried question. "Has anybody seen Gabriel?"

"Gabriel!" Lefty shouts up the stairs. "Where you at?"

"He's got the flag," I realize. "We've got to find him. Hey, *Duncan*! Is Gabriel up there with you?"

"Nope," Steve calls from far above. My envy starts to outweigh my fear. I'm going to climb.

"I'm down here, fellas." Gabriel's disembodied voice echoes up the stairwell.

I edge over to the abyss, more concerned about collaps-

THE SURFACE OF NEW YORK, in the summer of 2001, is a thriving human locus to rival any in history. The city encompasses 3.5 million tourists and commuters and 8 million residents on an average weekday, for a population density of 8,000 persons per square mile. The typical New Yorker, if he is a man, is among the most potent in America (sperm count 131.5 million). If a woman, she is among the most beautiful and sophisticated.

The city displays unprecedented highs and lows. It is the financial capital of the world, home of the planet's two largest stock markets. Still, some 30 percent of New Yorkers remain below the poverty line.

Art is dead. Conceptual art functions as editorial cartoon, lacking only punch-line captions. In architecture, postmodern attempts to retreat from austere modernism have been busier, but no less ugly, than their monolithic forebears. Confusion and inexpert fabrication are equally evident in the fashion industry. In 1950, the meanest laborer would scarcely consider leaving home without a jacket, tie, and hat. Today, attorneys and businessmen slouch into their high-rent offices dressed for the beach.

PURGATORY:
THE HIVE
PART II

FIVE INTO THE BREACH:
SMALLPOX HOSPITAL

Mission	
	SMALLPOX HOSPITAL, EARLY SUMMER 2001
Location	
	ROOSEVELT ISLAND
Goal	
	ENTER, EXPLORE
Officers	
	LEFTY LEIBOWITZ, L. B. DEYO
Team	
	STEVE DUNCAN, NICK SCIENCE, BRAZEN, SPECIAL AGENT RENÉE, GABRIEL, BRAIN, JOSH
Observers	
	BRAD WIENERS, KIKÉ ARENAL (*OUTSIDE* MAGAZINE)

Attach label, or print or type

REPORTED BY

L. B. Deyo

L. B. Deyo

What are the roots that clutch, what branches grow
Out of this stony rubbish?

T. S. Eliot, *The Waste Land*

A FURIOUS CROSSWIND rakes the low ground, churning the tall grass. The sky broils red across the skyline. Rain's coming, but not yet. We're inside the fence, past the lunar scars of the construction site, rounding the bend by the southwestern shore of Roosevelt Island, headed for the tree line that conceals the target. We move in loose formation. Steve Duncan is in front, rocking the Kool Moe Dee terminators, almost breaking stride. Close behind him marches Lefty Leibowitz in his shirtsleeves, sweating off the flu, joking with the Arch-Agent Gabriel. Josh hauls thirty pounds of camera equipment and roasts in his black suit, loving every second, and behind him Renée gracefully negotiates the black uneven ground, her hair braided down her back, sunglasses on. *Outside* magazine has sent along the Brobdingnagian Brad Wieners, six foot six and sunburned, blond ponytail, face scarred by adventure, and Kiké Arenal, his Venezuelan photographer, who ten days from now will be chasing down guerrillas in the Colombian jungle. Brazen hustles silently behind them, his face, as always, set in an impassive half-smile. Nick Science tries to raise headquarters on the handheld as I argue with Brain.

"The *McDonald's*!" Brain clutches at his midsection. He's dazed, unshaven, his shades missing. He winces at the ground.

"It was the only thing around," I say. "You should—"

"The only *what* around?" he shrieks. "Not *restaurant*. The place isn't fit for criminals!"

"Stop that, will you? What are you doing?" I hiss, lowering my outstretched hand to push down the volume. "Those construction trailers still have lights on. There could be people—"

"They'll never get us all," Nick says.

Brain defies me, pitching his voice higher. "I'm *poisoned*!" he moans. "God help me. It was the *beef*!" He stops dead in his tracks and lifts his plaintive eyes to heaven.

"You're not *poisoned*, Brain—"

"*Not poisoned?*" He coils as if to strike, then sags under the weight of his infirmity. "How can *you* know? Have you ever eaten anything that wasn't—Christ, I'm talking to an Irishman about *food*! Listen, my insides can't handle McDonald's. I'm not accustomed to eating *garbage* from a pig's *trough*!"

I have to stop my hand from clamping his mouth shut. The nearest trailer is just a few yards away. Pedestrians are strolling just outside the fence. "Okay," I say. "Renée has some Alka-Seltzer in her bag, I think. You should—"

"Alka Seltzer!" Brain snarls. "The fourth course in the *American meal*!"

"Brain, it'll straighten you right out."

Brain plants his feet and juts his chin out. "You couldn't get me to—*Alka*-Seltzer? Are you crazy?" His voice, lower now, retains its menace. "If you had *ten men* holding me down you couldn't force Alka-Seltzer down my throat. Christ, talk about poisoning—you think I'm going to swallow some weird *mineral*? And nobody really even knows *what* the stuff does to your insides—"

"There it is." Steve Duncan interrupts with a shout from the front of the pack. Turning the corner first, he sees the hospital rearing up against the sky. "Smallpox Hospital," Steve says, "one hundred and fifty years later."

So it is, unwrapped before us like a candy. Smallpox Hospital, the only official New York landmark in ruins, the city's best example of Gothic Revival, the crown jewel of Roosevelt Island. Its face glows in the floodlights, lit up for the commuters on the FDR Drive. Steel beams prop up the masonry. The whiteness of the façade sets off empty windows; it looks like a face with the eyes torn out, an empty skull.

"Stay out of the light," I say. "We can enter from the back."

Everybody picks up the pace now, charging through the damp grass, holding to shadows. The hospital is immense. Already we can see how wild the ruins have become, how densely overgrown. Trees rise sixty and seventy feet up from the rubble of the basement. Nine agents in uniform, with Brad and Kiké close at hand, swing around to the unlit lawn at the Queens side. We head inside the building.

There's not much of an "inside" left to the hospital. A full acre of roof and most of the upper floors are gone. As we enter the ruins, we see Manhattan through the hospital's heavy-lidded eyes, church windows full of light and inspiration. Halogen rays stream through a neglected scaffolding that reaches up five stories into the spires. Everybody's shooting now. Josh and Kiké's shutters chatter, their flashbulbs strobe the brick walls. Renée snaps an empty doorway forty feet above her, nothing on either side of it but treetops.

"Careful," says Renée. She holds the hem of her black dress now, peering intensely at the shifting bricks beneath her feet as we cross through an archway into what had been an adjacent room. The rubble piles up against the wall in a small hill. Half-buried doorways lead down into darkness. At the far side of the room, at the top of the pile, a wooden beam leads down from the second story. Duncan, still at point, reaches the beam first and effortlessly spirits himself up. Now on the second floor, he can peer down to survey the scene. In the closing decades of the nineteenth century, one of every hundred New York deaths happened here, in this broken fortress. Tonight, the flora strangle one another for every inch of earth. The trees spread up and out, attacking the walls as they once destroyed the roof. The greenery whips in the rising wind, flashing electric in the floodlights.

"See how the leaves are upturned?" Renée points for me. "That's the storm coming."

THE STAIRCASE

Duncan can't hear her. He's already inching up the shattered remains of a staircase. The first flight of stairs hangs from the wall in pieces, loose and gapped as a prizefighter's teeth. He grips the metal casements that bolt the stairs to the wall and splays himself like a spider to keep his weight off the steps. He moves quickly and automatically. The basement below him is a void; he can't even tell how far down it goes. Reaching the first landing, he sees he's only past the easy part. The next flight has no steps at all; only a wood plank connects his landing to the next one up.

"Jesus, are those stairs?" Brain asks, now inside.

"They used to be," I say. Then I shout up to Duncan, "Be very careful. At the first sign of collapse, I want to hear you say your prayers."

Duncan doesn't bother to look. He's on the second landing now, settling against it, testing its strength. Still no way to tell how high up he is: at least thirty feet, and the landing has no supports at all.

"That way," I continue, "I'll know you've gone to your reward with a clear conscience."

"And we'll be able to get out from underneath you," says the Brain.

Behind us, Gabriel has entered a side chamber with Lefty and Josh. "This is the autopsy room," he guesses. The floor and walls are tiled, and faucets stab out at unnatural angles. The clinical purpose still shows through fifty years of dust and graffiti. You can see the ghosts of doctors scrubbing up here, sterilizing their instruments. But the illusion ends at the fourth wall or, rather, the yawning hole where the fourth wall once stood. Josh strides to the edge of the floor, letting his gaze drop into yet another basement. The trees and shrubs grow thick down there. Josh says it looks like a jungle.

"It's like Maurice Sendak," says Gabriel. *"Where the Wild Things Are."* He pronounces the title respectfully, and we nod in agreement. The ruins recall the dreamscape of the children's story, where the boy's bedroom changes in the darkness. His carpet turns to grass, his closet becomes the mouth of a cave, and wild palms lilt in the starlight.

Brain stands behind them, looking over their shoulders, none the worse for wear. I congratulate him on surviving his Big Mac.

Brain's our own Falstaff: "Wherein cunning but in craft, wherein crafty but in villainy." He lights a cigarette and scowls at me. "Listen, I have a very delicate stomach," he says. "What about you? What's your excuse?"

Excuse for what, I ask him.

"*Ah*, you looked depressed at dinner!" he says. "You didn't even talk to Renée! I thought maybe you'd missed your *Prozac*!"

I tell him I'm fine. "Those customers in the McDonald's got on my nerves."

Brain hadn't noticed the people in the McDonald's. All he remembers is that *special sauce*—

"Just some Lower East Side clowns," I say. "Hipsters, you know. Pretty boys."

Brain's gaze drifts back into the trees as he nods and inhales a Pall Mall.

"Same type as we got taking over the whole city," I say. "Featherweights. Fashion guys. Curly-haired kids. The same downtown punks who been moving in since I got my apartment."

Brain stands silent, his eyes glazing over in the darkness. Is he still with me? He's just staring down into the jungle. Then he says, "Yeah?"

"Yeah. Well, you *asked*." I hate it when Brain asks a question and then fades out during my answer. Been doing it since we were in grade school. "I shouldn't let them get to me, right? I shouldn't rent them space in my head, I know. But they *ruin everything*. I mean, what are we doing here? We're here because this is a magnificent city, a city in stately decline. When I walk down the street, I want to enjoy the aesthetic. I want to feel the history. And how *can* I? The romance of the experience, you see, is spoiled because on every corner stands some lily-white swain with his lush, flowing locks and his semi-tinted '70s cop shades. It spoils it, because what's the point of being here if it's all just mall rats and club kids? Do you see what I mean? This was the city of Fitzgerald, E. B. White, Cab Calloway, Run-DMC, the Ramones, Dutch Schultz, Meyer Lansky, Alexander Hamilton, Aaron *Burr*, for God's sake. This was Damon Runyon's city! This was Babe Ruth's city. And now these *waifs* are inheriting it!"

"You're obsessed, Laughing Boy."

"Well, God *damn it!*" I implore him. "It's different where you live. In Astoria you've got families of *immigrants*, proud people, hardworking people. Manhattan kids are straight out of a music video. I mean, they rock their faded Smiths T-shirts and cutoff shorts. They go to the same beauty parlors as their girlfriends and walk out with Gabe Kaplan afros. And you think I'm crazy, but they all cultivate this kind of *socialist mystique*, carrying a copy of *Manufacturing Consent* in one hand and an iced coffee in the other, talking on a cell phone. Most of them are petty *traitors*. Sure, you say. But has it occurred to you that these people are a kind of vampire? See, I think that's why they all look so pale and weak. They come to New York and sink their fangs, and they bleed everything white. To walk through the Lower East Side these days, really, *you could almost be in L.A.*"

Brain laughs. "Laughing Boy, do you want to know the real reason you do this urban exploration?"

Preaching has worn me out; I have to catch my breath. "Yeah, what's that?"

"You love buildings," he says, "and you hate people."

CHALLENGE

"My adventures with Jinx have me convinced that its members could use a few days in the climbing gym— they are clumsy at best. . . ."

Brad Wieners, "Wild in the Streets," *Outside* **magazine**

"Hey there." Steve startles us by sticking his head down through a hole in the ceiling. "I think I've found a way to the roof. There's reinforced concrete all the way over—"

"Reinforced!" Brain shouts. "That's a relative term!"

"—it goes all the way over to the other wing, and then stops. I'm going to check it out." His head disappears into the ceiling.

"Stay close to the wall," I call after him. "The floor's weakest near the center, I think."

We turn back into the hallway, where the stairwell dares us to climb. Brazen has been rooting around below, and now catches up with us. "How did he get up there?"

"Took the stairs," I say.

"*Those* stairs?"

Nick Science jumps in at the dramatic pause to ask a worried question. "Has anybody seen Gabriel?"

"Gabriel!" Lefty shouts up the stairs. "Where you at?"

"He's got the flag," I realize. "We've got to find him. Hey, *Duncan*! Is Gabriel up there with you?"

"Nope," Steve calls from far above. My envy starts to outweigh my fear. I'm going to climb.

"I'm down here, fellas." Gabriel's disembodied voice echoes up the stairwell.

I edge over to the abyss, more concerned about collapsing the floor than falling off. "You're in the *basement*?" I can't believe it. It's pitch black down there. "Listen, can you toss me the flag?"

"Here you go," Gabriel shouts.

I shine my flashlight down into the cellar, surprised by how deep it is, how far below me Gabriel stands. The light catches the gleam in his sunglasses, the color of his tie, and then a movement as the Arch-Agent tosses up the flag. I grab it.

Gabriel doesn't use his flashlight unless he has to. He's run enough missions in populated areas to know their drawbacks. They spoil your night vision, of course, and they give your position away to anybody nearby. Worse, the damned things just aren't *stylish*, and Gabriel leads with his style.

I stand at the edge, still looking down. I start to unfold the flag, when my body jerks back on a reflex, dodging a plank of falling slate that smashes to the basement floor.

"Holy *shit*!" Brain shouts, staring at Nick, whose foot has just punched through the staircase and dislodged the step.

Nick steadies himself, gripping the landing with both hands. He carefully extracts his leg from the hole in the staircase. His face is blank.

"I'm not going up there," Josh declares. "I'm not doing it. Nick, be careful. Gabriel's in the basement right underneath you, and that landing's looking like it's going to collapse—"

"Yes," Nick cuts him off. "I had *noticed.*"

A fast pulse thrums across my temples, and my face spikes with heat. This has been the operation's closest call. That stair must have weighed thirty pounds at a

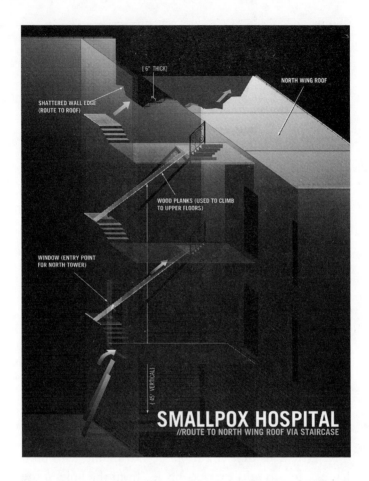

SHATTERED WALL EDGE
(ROUTE TO ROOF)

[6" THICK]

NORTH WING ROOF

WOOD PLANKS (USED TO CLIMB
TO UPPER FLOORS)

WINDOW (ENTRY POINT
FOR NORTH TOWER)

[45° VERTICAL]

SMALLPOX HOSPITAL
//ROUTE TO NORTH WING ROOF VIA STAIRCASE

minimum. It would have dashed my brains, or Gabriel's, had we been unlucky by inches. Nick is incomprehensibly cool, already continuing up the staircase, steady as iron. Nothing in his expression says he just almost plunged into a dark stairwell.

"I just want to know how Steve got up there," Josh says. "He just jetted on up, right when we got here."

Brain stands in the corner, tugging at his necktie.

"Some men hold their lives cheap," he says. "Steve's a man of action, totally fearless. A *moron*, in other words."

"What about you?" Brazen says. "Not here for the adventure?"

"Adventure?" Brain spits. "Is that what this is? Come on. Look at the graffiti on these walls. This isn't the Nile source, my friend. This is a *hangout* for *teenagers!*"

I have to answer him, but I don't want to. I'm shaken up. "An adventure can happen anywhere," I tell Brain. "What does it matter who's been here before? What difference does it make if teenagers make out in the basement and write their names on the wall? Most great discoveries have been made in inhabited lands. Even the Nile source, which you mention, was no empty waste when Speke and Burton found it. There were people there, ordinary people, doing ordinary, prosaic things. What about Columbus? Marco Polo? They discovered not empty deserts but great civilizations—"

"Marco Polo!" Brain can't contain himself. "A daring comparison!"

"I didn't mean—"

"—and *this* must be the court of Kublai Khan!" he cries. "Better not tell the vagrants, who use it as a *urinal!*"

"Brain, *keep your voice down*," Lefty snaps. "There might be workers around."

But Brain has tuned into his own private frequency. His stare lifts again to the sky, piercing through the obscuring clouds into the rolling wheel of space. "What an achievement," he says, "to have traveled great distances (on the subway!) and discovered this uncharted place. They'll write songs about this night. Our names will ring through the ages: The Jinx Project, *which discovered a building already known to every tourist with a guidebook."*

PHILOGENESIS

Everybody stands there in the silence after Brain's remarks.

Finally, I say, "I'm going up."

As I start my own climb, close at Nick's heels, Brazen strolls over and says, "You know what fascinates me about this railing?"

I'm on all fours, climbing toward the first landing of the staircase, staring down through the hole left by Nick's unlucky step. I'm disinclined to turn and reply to Brazen. His question strikes me as a bit abstract under the circumstances. I grunt.

"We were discussing complexity." He shines his light on the cast-iron curves of the banister. "This is a good example. Zoom in. Take one curve of the railing. Do you realize what it took to make this? A million years of human evolution."

Complexity theory, very roughly, says that dynamic systems live between the two extremes of order and chaos and survive by fighting the pull of each. Complexity has broad applications. Complex systems are adaptive, able to evolve. Life itself arises in complexity, in the dynamic range between order and chaos. So does the beauty of urban decline, the battle between artificial design and natural decay.

"A million years of evolution to make this railing," Brazen says. "You need an entire industrial enterprise—steel, coke, mining—or you can't make it. You can chisel out a stone by yourself, but only an industrialized civilization can make a steel railing."

"That's a decorative railing," Nick warns me from over-head. "Decorative, meaning non-structural."

CHANGELING

In 1854, James Renwick was here to see this hospital open its doors to New York's smallpox victims. The contagion was burning through the city.

> Smallpox was always present, filling the churchyard with corpses, tormenting with constant fear all whom it had not yet stricken, leaving on those whose lives it spared the hideous traces of its power, turning the babe into a changeling at which the mother shuddered, and making the eyes and cheeks of the betrothed maiden objects of horror to the lover.
>
> T. B. Macaulay, *The History of England from the Accession of James II*

Smallpox is alive, like the trees and shrubs that have infected this hospital. It is a virus, called *variola,* one of the smallest organisms known, yet its influence on human history has been enormous. Smallpox conquered the Americas for Spain. The virus, brought by Columbus, reached North America before Europeans did; by the time Ponce de Leon landed at Florida, the aboriginal population had been nearly wiped out. In its proliferation, the virus leaped first from cattle to humans in 1600 B.C. It flourishes in the bloodstream, injecting its genetic code into the cells of the living host, blooming over skin in painful lesions. It kills whole cities at a time.

Its control, and eventual elimination, then, was a holy crusade. James Renwick saw the sacred in his work. He was the architect of Grace Church and St. Patrick's Cathedral. All of his buildings, save this hospital, remain in use. This is Gothic Revival in the dark center of epidemic, amid the primitivism of nineteenth-century medicine. Renwick's hospital is like a church, with a cross at its central spire.

Vaccination conquered smallpox, long after the hospital shut its doors. To survive, an organism must be fruitful. Whether a breed of elephant or a bacterial strain, any species must be populated to a certain concentration if it is to reproduce successfully. If the concentration falls below that critical level, the species is doomed, even when individual specimens survive. To eradicate smallpox, it wasn't necessary to cure every single case on earth. The doctors needed only reduce its prevalence below that critical point. Though many still carried it, and some would yet die of it, smallpox by the 1950s was a dead species.

Today, it threatens us again. Two viable strains hibernate in the vaults of the U.S. and Russian disease centers, retained as weapons, and also as a seed for vaccine in case of emergency. At the Pentagon, strategists play out war game scenarios, running computer simulations of bioterrorist attack. They study the results and calculate losses of life, degrees of preparedness, methods of response. Their most deadly scenario, called "Dark Winter," is the smallpox attack.

ACROPHOBIA

Buildings, shimmering fabrics, woven of rich glass, to harmonize with the metal tracery to hold all together, to be a thing of delicate beauty, expressing the nature of that construction in the mathematics of structure. . . .

Frank Lloyd Wright, 1928

The third-floor landing abuts a brick wall whose upper edge is smashed. The edge rises in a jagged row of loose bricks to the roof. On the far side of the wall lies a long, sorrowful drop into the darkness of a courtyard. I hold my breath and lunge toward the wall, gripping it with both arms. I don't want to rest on the landing for even a moment; I've just seen it from below and it is unsupported. I feel the looseness of the wall.

The idea of climbing along this wall's top, up a pile of unattached bricks, is preposterous. Had I reached this point first, I would have declared it impassable, and headed back without loss of honor. Unfortunately, I am here *fourth*. Nick, Kiké, and Steve are already up and now chat pleasantly on the roof.

I pull myself up and sit on the wall, with a leg hanging down on each side. I use my hands to scoot along, gripping with my knees for balance. Kiké notices me.

"Are you going to hang the flag?" he asks, fingering the greedy lens of his camera.

Why do people keep trying to converse with me at these moments? My fingernails scrape into the bricks' chipped clay. For every inch I advance, the wall takes its toll against my groin. "Yes," I exhale. "I'm going to hang the flag."

Duncan waits in a Washingtonian posture; his rowboat across the Delaware is the edge of the hospital roof. He's been plotting routes to the building's front. The roof survives in sections; we're on the largest one, with an area of maybe seven hundred square feet, covering the northeast wing of the hospital. I stand beside Duncan and stare at the steeple, which adorns the western-facing front of the building. It stands with its solitary cross, silhouetted by the floodlights beyond. It's the highest point in the building, where we'll want to hang the flag. As the crow flies, it's all of two hundred feet away. Trouble is, we can't fly.

"What do you think?" I ask Steve.

"Well, there's no roof between here and the front. I think the only way to get there is to move along the tops of the walls, which are only about two feet wide. The mortar's deteriorated and the crenellations are kind of loose." (Crenellations form the distinctive pattern in the tops of castle towers and chess rooks.) He points to a wall that connects the rear to the front of the hospital. "If you've got more starch than me, you can follow that support wall across to the front, and that'll get you to the high point. Even if you get to the tower, though, it's kind of worrisome—"

"—it's kind of worrisome just standing here," I say.

"Well, it's worrisome because the whole thing is just sort of *stacked*. I think it's just gravity holding the front together at this point."

My face bunches up with grief. "I'll try the center wall," I hear myself saying. "Going to be a long crawl. I hope she's solid all the way."

Steve wishes me luck and heads back for the stairs. "I'm going to try that scaffolding as an alternate route, in case you can't make it."

I kneel down and gently let myself fall forward into the top of the rear wall. I seem to be higher than before—six stories? seven?—the ground must be lower in the back. The wall's surface is about as broad as my shoulders. That could be worse, but the battlements are hidden beneath a dense growth of ivy, so I can't make out the peaks and valleys. I have no way of judging the wall's state of repair. Faith is the evidence of things unseen.

The wall offers a privileged vantage. I'm looking down

into a cross section, a breakaway diagram of nineteenth-century building arts. This is the advantage of collapse. No one who walked the halls of this building when it was new and whole could see what I see now: the seams of the floor, the mixture of the concrete, the bones of the structure in a one-to-one scale model.

The death struggle stands frozen around me. It is a memory, imperfectly preserved. Smallpox Hospital began as an idea, expressed on blueprints in ideal vectors on the Euclidian plane. The idea took shape through the skillful fashioning of brick and mortar. The human cerebrum also builds ideas as physical structures, intricate nets of neural growth around reinforced information loops. The senile brain disintegrates; memories die as spider webs pulled apart in widening gaps and snapping threads. Now I see James Renwick's idea dying. It falls away piecemeal with every brick.

The seagulls arrive, screaming across the sky like fighter-bombers, driven crazy by the smell of the gathering storm.

Renée, Lefty, and Brazen stand on the grounds outside the hospital, looking up at me. Across the eastern water, a neon Pepsi sign throws its garish red over the river. Strange, to be here in this overgrown romantic glade, yet still surrounded by a living city. Brazen points a cigarette's glowing tip at me and says something to Lefty.

I look down into the building again. What looks like a floor below is really the canopy of treetops. I feel around blindly for each solid grip as I crawl. A bunch of ivy breaks off in my hands, and I fall on my face, cursing, "*Idiot.* Risking my life here, for what? Is this the court of Kublai Khan?"

I reach the south end of the rear wall. Now I scramble

up onto the roof of the south wing, wrestling the damp vines. This roof has fared even worse than the north wing's; it's ragged, like the edge of a half-burnt map. I-beams show scandalously through, crisscrossed above the gloom of another verdant basement. It's reassuring to be back on a roof—even this roof. Maybe if I stay above the I-beams, I'll have less chance of falling through. Small trees, rooted in the tiles, grow here far above the ground. I push my way through them, my back scraping along the parapet. The branches are so thick I can neither walk nor crawl; I have to twist myself into the empty spaces, half-climbing, shoving myself forward with my feet. I wonder, as I near the hospital front where the team waits for me, whether I'll hear a creaking sound before the roof collapses.

"There he is!" Brain shouts as he sees me appear over the high side. "Don't worry, Laughing Boy, we'll catch you if you fall!"

I drag myself up onto the edge of the front wall, exhausted and relieved. After a moment to restore the breath to my lungs, it's time to represent.

"That's perfect!" Renée shouts, focusing her camera. "You look great! You're all lit up against the sky!"

"There's Steve, too," says Nick Science, pointing.

Sure enough, Steve is also in full view, also lit up as though onstage as he climbs the façade. He can't see me above him. He's focused on each handhold and foothold.

Taking a last look back as I unfurl the flag, I shudder at the devastation. These walls were meant as a bulwark against death. The hospital was an inverse fortress, protecting the world outside from an enemy within. Smallpox is a childhood disease, and the children who slept here knew their chances. They knew they were quarantined not for themselves but for the good of others. Did they sit up in their beds at night and peer out the caged windows, past the shores of Roosevelt Island and across the river to Manhattan?

Now the walls are open. The fortress is breached and overrun. The battle of Renwick Hospital is the same as every battle: walls are built, walls are broken through. I turn to face the team. Everyone stands arrayed down there, eyes locked on the banner. Slowly I straighten up in the wind, six stories in space, waving the Jinx flag to say the castle has fallen.

SIX GHOSTS OF HARLEM: ⚠
THE ABANDONED ROW HOUSE

Mission		CONDEMNED BUILDING, LATE SUMMER 2001
Location		EAST HARLEM
Goal		EXPLORE A CONDEMNED BUILDING
Officers		LEFTY LEIBOWITZ, L. B. DEYO
Team		JOSH, MIKE

Attach label, or print or type

REPORTED BY

L. B. Deyo

L. B. Deyo

THE CAPSULE

Traveling into the city as a kid, I rode the Metro-North commuter trains on the Hudson line. The route went down the river to the Bronx, where it veered into the city across elevated tracks. For forty blocks or so, before plunging into the Grand Central tunnels, the train would snake through Harlem.

To me, a Westchester teenager, New York offered an irresistible cocktail of fear and grandeur. It lured as much by its dangers and squalor as by its riches. And what was true of New York generally was doubly true of Harlem, perhaps its most famous neighborhood. Here was another world, celebrated and reviled, dreaded for crime, poverty, and unrest, famed for art, music, literature. Like the whole city in concentrate, it encompassed the best and worst of America. Everyone knew of Harlem's agony: Murder, arson, riots, and disease dominated news coverage of the neighborhood. By 1990, *The New England Journal of Medicine* would report that Harlem's men had shorter life expectancies than those of Bangladesh. Yet this was nothing like the stereotypical ghetto: Harlem had clout and mystique, earned through almost a century at the hot center of American life. It had played a central role in the nation's political, social, and artistic life. It was the birthplace of the NAACP, Marcus Garvey's Universal Negro Improvement Association, the Harlem Renaissance, the Savoy Stomp, Ralph Ellison's *Invisible Man*, and stride piano. In an American century, Harlem had left its mark on every corner of the world.

Of the Harlem I could see from the air-conditioned safety of the train, nothing was more fearful and intriguing than its condemned buildings. Whole blocks stood shuttered up and abandoned. Many houses and tenements, haunted masterpieces of late-nineteenth-century architecture, remained beautiful in their death masks. Though forbidding, wreathed in razor wire, with windows boarded shut and doorways walled with brick and mortar, the buildings showed signs of ingress and egress. There was life hidden within.

Even then, a young kid looking out from the window of a train, I wanted to see into those buildings. My imagination was fueled by tabloid headlines and secondhand accounts. I was sure that horrors, real horrors, waited inside: deranged squatters and addicts crouched in darkness, syringes and crack vials strewn over the rotting floors. Yet even years later I couldn't shake the desire to find out for sure, because it was dangerous, because no one I knew of had ever done it. And I hoped that by exploring one of these ghost houses, I, an outsider, might discover some essence of this neighborhood. Harlem waited there, strange as the surface of Mars, close as the outside of the windowpane.

BROKEN GLASS, EVERYWHERE

"Lot of opportunities," Josh says, looking out from the backseat. "Look at that red building. No glass in the windows, ground floor's all boarded up."

"Damn." Mike nods. "It's a beautiful building, too."

"It's too close to the police station," Lefty says. "We don't want the law to see us."

The 28th Precinct building blazes white in the withering sunshine. It's low-slung, built in the brutalist style that four decades ago would have been called futuristic. In a district of subtle curves and elegant limestone façades, the station is a squat, ugly fortress. Where brownstones and churches have grown organically into a neighborhood, the precinct house slammed down like a boot.

The paramilitary redoubt stands as a crisis frozen in mortar. Its crudeness of design, its right angles and indecorous face express a retreat from chaos. When they built it in 1974, the government created, instead of a community police station, a base behind enemy lines.

Lefty grips the wheel of his truck, scanning the street signs. We're roving through the heat of a midafternoon in Harlem, scouting for a target.

THE ROW HOUSE

We round the corner of 122nd Street, and everybody sees it at once. "That one," Josh says, jabbing a finger toward a five-story brownstone. The building is shut up, webbed with scaffolding, but its elegance is undiminished. It has a raised basement, a high, heavy stoop with balustrade and cast-iron railings. The facing is Jersey freestone, a rich brown with weathered mortar. The windows and doorway are hooded, and the whole structure stepped back to an overhanging roof. This is no tenement, but a fine single-family home, probably built in the first three decades of the twentieth century. Josh is halfway out of the truck with his camera ready before Lefty can pull up beside a fireplug.

"Kind of small." Mike follows, slamming the door behind him. "Looks like it's under construction. We better make sure there's no hard hats working here."

"It's perfect," I say. It's not a sealed vault, like many abandoned buildings, but if anything this makes it more interesting. The scaffolding will allow access to the upper structure, and the unshuttered windows will give us light.

A vacant lot lies adjacent, fenced off with a chain-link fence. Lefty locks the truck and follows us around to see the side. The lot has a dirt floor. There's a Dumpster and another tower of scaffolding rising all the way to the roof.

I strain to see through the empty window frames; there doesn't appear to be anything inside above the second floor. "I think the whole thing is hollowed out," I say. "It's just an empty shell, with no floors."

"Check it out, I guess." Lefty looks around. His brow is knitted with concern, or maybe the glare. "You see those people over there, right?"

I'm already climbing over the fence. "Yeah, I saw them."

Lefty's trying to play it off, but he can't stop glancing to his right. There are five middle-aged guys playing dominoes on a folding card table. They're on the sidewalk in front of a social club, not fifty feet from us. They converse in Spanish. Other men, and a woman, keep coming out of a door to talk to them.

"You think they saw you?" Lefty asks me as I make a hard landing on the dirt inside the fence.

"No," I lie. "They can't see around that wall. If you guys just climb right here, at the edge of the fence, you won't be spotted."

I've ripped my jacket again. There's got to be a suit out there that can stand up in the field, but I'm not wearing it. I run back into the vacant lot and duck behind the Dumpster. I scan the windows of the surrounding buildings to see if anybody's looking down.

Close up, I can see into the building. The ground floor is a maze of wreckage: Old furniture, lamps, and fixtures lean against walls that have holes big enough to walk through. The floorboards are torn up, and cables hang from the ceilings.

I call out to the guys, "It looks good. We'll enter here, from the scaffolding. Come on, let's get it done."

As Mike and Josh scramble over the fence, Lefty takes a last look over at the dominoes game. Something about the way the card table shudders when a player slams down his tile makes Lefty miss his stride. "Damn," he mutters, digging the toe of his wingtip into the fence. An old player meets his gaze, then looks down again at the game.

EMPIRICISM

The only weapon we have in our exploration is the discipline of empiricism. Our picture of the world is mere speculation, rumor, until grounded in direct observation. We'll test my lurid imaginings, dreamed of on hermetic commuter trains. It's time to leave the capsule, if I dare.

The ground floor is gutted. The intestine secrets of the structure spill out in a tangle of pipes, wires, and splintered wood. A rubble of Sheetrock, bricks, and garbage slows our progress. Large holes in the floor reveal a basement, but it's too dark to see what's down there.

There's a small kitchen, discernible as such only by the linoleum floor. The counters are gone. Some of the cabinets and a sink lie piled in a corner. The air is stale. The blend of house dust and urine makes my eyes water. It's ninety degrees.

A small bedroom lies beyond the kitchen. Cigarette butts are scattered across the floor. A single page from a magazine hangs by a tack on the wall: It's an advertisement showing a businessman with a sumo wrestler sitting on his shoulders.

Through a tear in the ceiling, we see the roof, four stories above. It's clean blond wood, probably only weeks old. Someone has invested in this property. We head out onto the scaffolding and scale up to the second floor to take in the rest of the building.

Stepping in through the window, Lefty places his right foot gently on the second floor. He keeps his weight on his back foot, still safely anchored on the windowsill. Gripping the edge of the frame, he eases forward, trusting more and more of his mass to the surface. He breathes in hot air and lets his gaze shuttle across the whole subjected plane. It's a shattered waste, piled high along the edges with construction debris, worn through in patches close to the center. Finally, he lifts his back foot from the windowsill and steps forward, entirely supported by late-nineteenth-century workmanship.

"Not what you'd expect, is it?" Lefty says.

"It's unreal." I nod, following him into the mammoth chamber, taking it all in. What was from without a row house is from within a cathedral. Sunlight pours in from the afternoon sky, igniting the falling dust. The west side of the building is closed; whatever windows were once there have been painted over or nailed shut. The front of the building has six high columns of windows, silhouetting the space between them. Seven more columns run along the east wall, each column four windows high. Every single window is an empty space; not a single pane of glass remains.

This second floor isn't a floor at all, we realize. We're standing on the ceiling of the rooms below. "Be careful," says Lefty.

We hold back at first, moving along the wall, where the ceiling is likely to be stronger. The limitations of the structure express themselves as a huge crater in the center, a hole big enough to drop a hatchback through.

There's a bathtub sitting against the eastern wall. It's a heavy one, solidly built. It's filled with pulverized Sheetrock and white dust. Against the western wall, the track of a dumbwaiter stretches all the way to the roof. The dumbwaiter itself is shredded, hanging limp from its housing.

Near the back of the building, a *Hustler* magazine lies on the floor. A methadone bottle stands near the corner, its label still legible, still containing a trace quantity of the drug. Beside it, a Polaroid shows three men posing before a brick wall. One of the men wears a Newport cigarette T-shirt that reads, "Alive with Pleasure."

I step out the rear window.

THE FIRE ESCAPE

What, in fire escapes, do I admire? Their universality: their equal utility across cities and neighborhoods; their economy of design: their rugged skeletal strength and transparent unity: their spontaneous novelty: the simply sturdy curves overlapping when viewed from a given vantage, filtering the masonry or brick: their constancy: sound as a dollar, firm as Gibraltar, unshaken by the decades, neglected yet shouldering their vital charge, clinging, like Ulysses to his barque, through hurricanes, freezing gales of winter: safely conducting bolts of lightning; supporting, as Atlas, the gravid snows of winter: the variation within an essential form, like the very snowflake, each unique yet all bound by unyielding laws of construction: their balance, supporting the disproportionate mass with the well-placed lever arm: their hospitality, Ralph and Alice being neither the first nor the last to avail themselves in the heat of summer, and this tradition remaining firmly in place throughout the urban world from East New York to Calcutta and Hong Kong: their elasticity: swelling in the humid summers, shrinking in winter months like the boards of the Ancient Mariner's ship: their uncomplaining servility in blurring uneventful years: their silent heroism in the teeth of a four-alarm blaze: their romantic accessibility, climbing from the sidewalk into the starry firmament.

EXISTENCE AND ESSENCE

In my wildest dreams I had anticipated none of this: the cavernous emptiness sliced by the streaming bands of sunshine, the wrecked dumbwaiter, the sumo wrestler pinned to the bedroom wall, the bathtub filled with dust. Nor could I have. The most reasoned speculations must always yield only the faintest approximation of what direct experience will show. The mission is accomplished, my ghosts dispersed by the light of observation.

As we head back to Lefty's truck, the domino players look up at us. Are they curious? Angry? Friendly? I turn away, somehow unable to return their gaze.

This is Harlem, once home to Marcus Garvey and Fletcher Henderson, W. E. B. Du Bois, Adam Clayton Powell, Malcom X. The most notorious gangsters of the century came here to exploit the neighborhood: Dutch Schultz, Lucky Luciano, Fidel Castro, Nikita Khrushchev. Others glorified the place by their very presence: Zora Neale Hurston, Langston Hughes, Lena Horne, Willie the Lion Smith, Cab Calloway, Duke Ellington, Louis Armstrong, and Martin Luther King, Jr. We stand in Harlem, unrivaled by any neighborhood as a shaper and source of American culture. It remains a thriving community, burgeoning with growth and life, in the midst of its greatest upswing since the Harlem Renaissance.

And what has our empiricism uncovered? Nothing. The cracks in the masonry held no residue of Harlem's glory, no trace of what Harlem means. Our row house was dead, empty, and silent. We've learned nothing about the neighborhood because a neighborhood is made not of concrete and glass but of people.

This is the weakness of urban exploration. Our only interaction with people is in avoiding them. We slip in and out like thieves, we cling to the shadows and avert our eyes, and so we study a city of buildings, a city of bridges and tunnels, but not a city of human beings. Millions live and work here, but the New York we explore is as empty as this building. We ourselves are the ghosts.

SEVEN DIPLOMACY:
THE UNITED NATIONS

Mission	TRILATERAL COMMISSION HQ, UNITED NATIONS
Location	MIDTOWN MANHATTAN
Goals	ENTER AND SURVEIL TRILATERAL HQ, HANG JINX FLAG IN FRONT OF UNITED NATIONS
Officers	LEFTY LEIBOWITZ, L. B. DEYO
Team	AGENT BLEACH, MIKE, SPECIAL AGENT RENÉE, JOSH

Attach label, or print or type

REPORTED BY

L. B. Deyo

L. B. Deyo

WE THE PEOPLES OF THE UNITED NATIONS DETERMINED to save succeeding generations from the scourge of war, which twice in our lifetime has brought untold sorrow to mankind, and to reaffirm faith in fundamental human rights, in the dignity and worth of the human person, in the equal rights of men and women and of nations large and small, and to establish conditions under which justice and respect for the obligations arising from treaties and other sources of international law can be maintained, and to promote social progress and better standards of life in larger freedom. . . .

> **Preamble to the United Nations Charter, October 24, 1945**

I SHOW UP at three in the afternoon with Josh and Mike. Bleach stands waiting for us on the corner of 45th and First, nodding his head as we approach. He's mint condition, as usual; face impassive as the granite wall he leans on, shirt gleaming behind the flawless black suit and tie. Eighty-five degrees out, Bleach is cool, not sweating a damn thing. "You made it." He nods to us.

Née appears from around the far corner. Her hair and skin are burnished in the sunshine. She's sipping at a straw and smiling at me. Her gait is playful; she almost skips over as she greets us.

Lefty arrives last, tugging at his collar and wincing in the glare. Reaching us, he narrows his eyes and takes the measure of our group. With a defiant flourish he removes his jacket. He turns an accusing eye toward me and asks if anybody remembered the flag.

I button up my own jacket, tug its bottom edge to smooth it, and tell him not to worry; I've got the flag. Then we all turn toward our objective. And there it is, filling the eastern sky, the United Nations building; a mirrored vault against the East River, wreathed with blue. The broad Le Corbusier is one tremendous mother, offering freely the shelter of her bosom to 4,000 employees, 191 member states, and all the peoples of the world. Vertiginous, millennial, serene, the building, like her charter, is both a dream and a promise.

The United Nations was founded in 1945 with a modest purpose: saving succeeding generations from war, preserving the rights of man, meting out law and something called "social progress" to all humanity. In the decades since, the United Nations has amply proved the value of its utopian promise. Today's peaceful, lawful, progressive world, where violence and poverty exist only in history books, is largely the result of the United Nations' efforts. How many take the time to let them know how grateful they are?

We couldn't wait to let them know. So today we have come to hang the Jinx flag, right on their goddamn front lawn.

PREPARATIONS

Stealth offered the only hope for this assault on international soil. Only commando tactics could serve. We meant to run our flag up one of their own flagpoles; this would mean usurping some other nation's banner, in the very midst of those powder-blue-clad U.N. troops. The job called for one, maybe two operatives, dressed all in black and clinging to the shadows under cover of night. They'd have to crawl on their bellies up the shore from the river, slowing their breathing when a patrol came near, freezing for minutes at a time as flashlights skimmed across their backs. With no mistakes, they might have a chance at reaching the flagpole to complete the mission.

The others have vetoed this plan. They prefer that I should hang the flag, alone, not in the middle of the night but now, in broad daylight, in front of all the tourists. After all, the worst that could happen is that I'd get arrested, and they'd go get a late afternoon snack.

Josh and Mike will photograph the event from a safe distance. Née will provide close logistical support, escorting me into international territory. Bleach will stay close behind, providing security (that is, the kind of security one unarmed man, a known cross-dresser, can offer against several divisions of Peacekeepers and the NYPD). Lefty will command, leaving me free to do all the work. That, at least, is reassuringly familiar.

WE WERE IN THE NEIGHBORHOOD

"Do we hang the flag now?" Josh asks, loading his medium-format camera.

"First things first," I say. "We're going to drop in on the Trilaterals."

There was no way we could hit the United Nations, in an official diplomatic capacity, without stopping by the world headquarters of the Trilateral Commission. It would be like going to Disneyland without riding the Pirates of the Caribbean.

The Trilateral Commission is a serious body, and it does serious work. It's a nongovernmental organization made up of political leaders from a broad array of countries. It strives to smooth over international relations, provide a forum for the settlement of disputes, and help coordinate national economies. All of which is boring. What makes the Trilateral Commission attractive to us is its unique, if undeserved, infamy. The Trilaterals are the Beatles of the Conspiracy Fringe. Ask any lone gunman type about the commission, and the hair on the back of his neck will shoot up. The Trilaterals are routinely accused of everything from overthrowing the shah of Iran to handpicking every U.S. president since Carter to ruling the world. Following are some "Frequently Asked Questions" they feel obliged to answer in their press package:

- Is the Trilateral Commission trying to establish a world government?
- Is the Trilateral Commission a "club" for the benefit of rich countries only?
- Is the Trilateral Commission a conspiracy to control the U.S. government?
- How did it happen that President Carter chose seventeen of his top officials from the ranks of the Trilateral Commission?

Obviously, these are our kind of people.

The front entrance of Trilateral headquarters is closed for construction. We round the corner and head to the side entrance. Within the glass doors, two security guards and some clerical workers are waiting. Outside on the sidewalk, we form a huddle.

"What do you want to do?" Bleach says. "We can't sneak past those guards."

I don't answer. There's nothing to say, and we're already drawing attention to ourselves just standing there in our suits and shades. On Jinx missions it's more the rule than the exception that audacity is our only plan; the city is too fluid for prepared itineraries, even if we were diligent enough to make them.

I walk in the front door. The first guard's nameplate says, "Jenny." She looks at me like I've just stepped off a flying saucer. "Can I help you with something?"

"Yes," I say, flashing her a smile and a good look at herself in my shades. "I'm here for the Trilateral Commission."

"Uh-huh," she nods. Jenny wasn't born yesterday. "And you are?"

"My name is L. B. Deyo. I'm here from *Jinx* magazine." I only marginally focus on the conversation as I scan the room. The configuration of this makeshift lobby is unfortunate. The whole space isn't much larger than a child's bedroom. The walls are Sheetrock, the floor is bare concrete. Beyond the guard station, the elevators tantalize. Bleach is right: There's no way to sneak in.

"Yeah." Jenny is conversing with another guard. She turns to me and says, "You got an appointment?"

"No, I'm here to make an appointment. I want to schedule an interview—" My radio interrupts, squawking to life from my breast pocket. I nonchalantly shut it off.

"Okay." Jenny nods, picking up a phone receiver. "Let me call up, because they're going to have to send someone down to escort you. Hello?" she says into the phone. "Yeah, someone's here from—*Jet* magazine?"

"No, *Jinx*," I interrupt her. "*Jinx* magazine."

While she talks to the people upstairs, I duck out to fetch Josh. Lefty asks what's going on.

"They're sending someone down to escort me into the building. Josh, you come with me and shoot."

We head back inside to wait. Jenny has made me a

nametag and has me sign the register. She tells Josh he'll need a nametag too.

"So," says Jenny, leaning back against the Formica counter. "*Jinx* magazine." She's a big girl. She knows she could handle both of us if necessary. "Is that, like, *known*?"

Before I can answer, a small, hatchet-faced woman struts out from the elevator, wearing a business suit and holding a manila envelope. She looks me right in the face and says, "*George?*"

Josh and I look at each other. "No," I tell her.

The woman's face pulls back in disgust. She turns to Jenny for an explanation of this affront. "Where are they?"

"This is them," Jenny nods. She's having a great time.

"You're *not* from *George* magazine?" the woman asks me.

"We're from *Jinx* magazine," I say. "It's an online magazine dealing with—"

She scorches me with a vicious eye roll and shoves the envelope into my hand. "Here," she says, and turns back toward the elevator.

I try to stop her. "Yes, well, we were going to—"

She turns and pinches a smile. "*Good-bye.*"

Josh and I step back out into the sunshine. Even with my shades, the light is dazzling. Bleach, Lefty, Née, and Mike are waiting a few yards up the sidewalk.

"Well?" Lefty stares.

"It wasn't our finest hour," I tell him.

COFFEE BREAK

The Trilateral fiasco has been the operation's worst defeat. The situation calls for coffee—and plenty of it. We head around the corner to a glass kiosk and take one of the tables that surround it in the open air. Blaming myself for our humiliation, I offer to buy the first round. Bleach declines, Née and Mike ask for iced coffees. Josh wants a large black—his sixth of the day.

Lefty Leibowitz doesn't drink coffee. After sixteen years of friendship, this remains a barrier to my understanding of him. Like Josh, I hold coffee slightly less necessary than oxygen; I drink seven to ten cups on a typical day.

Inside the kiosk, I commit my second serious blunder of the mission: In retrospect, the error is attributable to my low caffeine levels (it's four hours since my last cup). A psychostimulant, caffeine improves concentration, recall, and mental performance, all of which, in me, are now found wanting. "Four iced coffees, please," I tell the vile-complexioned teen. "Two with milk, two black."

Outside, Josh accepts his order as he would a live hand grenade. A dog, if kicked, will look at his attacker with sharp apprehension, at once terrified, resentful, cautious, and enraged. "Dude," says Josh, setting down his cup, "I didn't want iced coffee. I wanted *hot* coffee."

Josh is a man of singular intelligence, a product of the prestigious Rochester University photography program. Unquestionably, his I.Q. is well above the average, but it decreases, temporarily, when he says "dude." How, if I.Q. is a measure of innate intelligence, can it so fluctuate? The answer is simple. I.Q., like any statistic, is properly a measurement rather than a material object. The whole mathematical field of statistics, no less the subfield of psychometrics, is predicated on the understanding that measurements are imperfect. That's why statistics deals with means and trends, degrees of confidence. A person's I.Q. is not his intelligence, only a measurement of his intelligence. The success of various I.Q. tests, and indeed the I.Q. concept, rests not on whether I.Q. corresponds to a real, physical "thing" in the brain, but how well it correlates to other related measurements.

Coffee increases I.Q. By sharpening concentration, recall, perceptions, and mental speed, it boosts subjects' performance on I.Q. tests. And there is literally no difference between "subjects' performance on I.Q. tests" and "subjects' I.Q.s."

Psychologists accept a range of I.Q. tests as valid. Some tests are formal, others, by necessity, far less so. A psychologist who must evaluate the intelligence of a subject in a hurried, nonclinical setting can do a highly casual I.Q. test in the form of a conversation. Vocabulary is more highly correlated with I.Q. than any other mental faculty, so simply by evaluating the vocabulary of a subject, the psychologist can find out his I.Q. Saying "Dude, I didn't ask for iced coffee" temporarily lowers Josh's apparent intelligence, therefore his I.Q. By way of ameliorating his temporary handicap, I hurry to get him a hot cup of coffee. It should do the trick.

When I return, I notice Bleach continues his cool appraisal of our little band, eyes inscrutable behind black lenses. Then, he amazes me by asking, "What exactly is it we have against the U.N.?"

This naked heresy, so calmly dispensed, runs through the team as a high-voltage current. Every eye fixes on him, and then, as abruptly, on me.

I take a sip of coffee and study Bleach's face for some hint of motive. Some questions, I tell myself, really are innocent. Nothing in his cordial gaze suggests a deliberate assault on the authority of the Project. In his three years of service, no charge of disloyalty has ever been whispered against him. In 1998, by way of initiating himself into Jinx service, Bleach willingly endured a trial by fire in the shape of his now famous 24-hour-subway odyssey. Eschewing the comforts of his bed, he armed himself with a camera and a supply of No-Doz and bought himself a token at five P.M.; he would not return to the natural light of the streets above until five P.M. the following day. For this service, he was in 1999 awarded the Medal of Courage by the Jinx Athenaeum.

Bleach's natural cunning, his innate sense of intrigue and secrecy, might have aroused Project suspicion. More than anything else, the Medal of Honor proudly worn at meetings had deflected such suspicion. Have we been fooled by our own prize? For this was not the first time Bleach had questioned the Enemies list. In late 1999, in an otherwise rousing speech against Walt Disney, Inc., Bleach had attacked Walt Disney for, of all things, his opposition to the United Nations. "What kind of man would oppose the U.N.?" he had asked. "An organization whose only goal is peace?" I had chalked it up to ignorance then. Bleach had simply not known our position, and had inadvertently opposed it. Now I wasn't so sure.

The others' faces tell me I must answer the question. My instinct tells me it's too late. A Project decision can never be questioned; this is axiomatic to our whole mission. By responding to the question, I confer legitimacy on it, and on the right of any agent, at any time, to ask his own questions. This would be the end of the Jinx Project.

If I sought guidance from Lefty, it was in vain. His face was as expectant as the others; indeed, there was a challenge in the arch of his eyebrows that was his alone. Was this a coup? Had I been set up? I looked to Née, calmly drinking her coffee. Could she, too, be involved? The bonds of our affection were strong, I believed. But what man is ever sure?

I must respond quickly, I know. Every second I delay weakens my position further. If this is a conspiracy, they will count on me to react with my usual bluster. So I call the bluff—I treat the question as innocently as it had, supposedly, been asked.

"The United Nations was supposed to be a tool, a service, to its member states," I tell Bleach, my voice steady. "For a while it was. But by the early sixties it had become an organ of world socialism, dominated by a bloc of Third World dictatorships, the so-called non-aligned movement. The worst tyrants on earth, from Nasser and Sukarno to Saddam Hussein and Ho Chi Minh, sent their emissaries to vote condemnations against the United States. The U.N. became ideologically opposed to Western democracy.

"The lowest point for the U.N. may have been the day Idi Amin came. This was 1975. Amin was dictator of Uganda and head of the Organization of African Unity. He came to the U.N. to denounce the 'Zionist U.S. conspiracy.' He called for genocide in Israel.

"This was a man who knew something of genocide. His government had murdered two hundred thousand Ugandans, some with sledgehammers. Amin didn't rely only on henchmen for this killing. He killed hundreds himself, in the torture chamber of his own palace. His victims were ritually tortured, castrated. He cannibalized many of them, including his wife and the heart of his son.

"Amin received a thunderous standing ovation that day at the U.N., because everything he stood for, everything he said in his speech, was representative of the U.N. majority. They were committed anti-Semites.

"They were anti-Western radicals who blamed the world's troubles on the United States. They had nothing bad to say about the Soviet Union, which had killed over twenty million people, or China, which had killed almost sixty million. The West was their scapegoat, and the stumbling block in their vision.

"After Amin's speech, he was honored by the secretary general and the president of the General Assembly at a public feast."

I exhale and wipe the sweat from my forehead with a paper napkin. I've indulged, again, the worst of my vices: speech making. As always, the experience leaves me shocked and embarrassed. It's a bit like coming out of a trance; I suddenly realize I'm half-shouting at a rapid clip and that everyone is staring at me. I almost apologize.

Bleach smiles. "That was twenty-five years ago." The son of a bitch. Is he baiting me, or am I imagining the whole thing?

"Yes," I reply, modulating my tone again, slowing down the words. "Some things have improved. But the problem with the U.N. is larger than individual incidents. Our entire constitution is based on the decentralization of power. We separate our government into state and federal, and each of these governments is further divided into legislative, judicial, executive. You see? The founders knew that decentralization would weaken the government, to the benefit of the citizens; they deliberately created a separation of power.

"The U.N. is based on an opposite philosophy. It seeks to establish international norms to which every government will be obligated. It attempts to assert sovereignty over national governments and create a central authority over the world. It does this by treaties, accords, and in extreme cases with the intervention of its own army, the peacekeepers—"

Lefty interrupts me. "The peacekeepers," he says, "are taking down the flags."

SECRETARIAT

So they are. Across the street, two U.N. officers in their powder-blue uniforms stroll down the line, stopping at each flagpole to lower the flags for the day.

"It's only four o'clock," Renée says. "There's still five hours of daylight. Why would they take them down now?" She's got her game face on, but I can tell she's dispirited. We all are. The Trilateral defeat was bad enough. But after our heated exchange, I feel demoralized, unsure of myself and the whole operation. Watching the flags drift limply down their poles, I feel myself weaken. If the team decides to abort, I don't know if I'll have the nerve to rally them.

Lefty stands up at this moment, his eyes boring into the U.N. Secretariat. He puts on his suit jacket and his sunglasses. Then he turns back to face us, sets his jaw, and says, "It doesn't change a thing. Let's do this."

And we're off—across the street, right through the traffic (let the sons of bitches swerve around us), heads high, eyes forward. Roll up on the main entrance, up the concrete steps, taking in all thirty-nine stories of mirrored windows and the blue sky reflected in them. Past the peacekeepers, who smile carelessly at us.

To our hard left at the top of the steps stands a low-slung concrete bunker, one man inside. The guards who were striking the flags have moved on—they've got dozens more to go, and each one will take them farther from us. I hustle around the back, noticing an open entrance in the bunker's rear. Renée and Bleach catch up with me.

"What do you think?" I ask.

"The guards are—" Bleach nods toward the steps, all of twenty feet away. "I think they're gonna see you."

"I know," I say, climbing nonchalantly over a yellow chain that ropes off the area. "But check it out. If none of them goes to the bottom of the stairs, I can run the flag up and they won't be able to see me." I point to indicate the guards' line of sight. "See? I don't think they'll be able to see the flag until it's at the top of the mast."

"What about all the tourists?" Renée looks around. We've got a little tree cover here at the edge of the U.N. campus, but we're fully exposed to the street. People are walking by close enough to reach out and touch, and they're already starting to notice us.

I get on the radio. "Mike, this is Laughing Boy. Come in."

"Roger, Laughing Boy. Mike here, go ahead."

We are grown men. "I need you and Josh to get to the sidewalk in front, just a bit south of the stairs at the campus entrance. We're going to make this happen, but it's going to be very quick and I need you ready to shoot."

"Copy that, Laughing Boy," Mike says. "We're way in the back, by the river. Give us five minutes to get to position, over."

I tell Bleach and Renée we've got five minutes.

"Let's look in the bunker," Renée says. She's inside before I can disagree.

The damn thing looks just like an imperial bunker, like

the one Han Solo had to blow up in *Return of the Jedi*. It was also under tree cover, on the Ewok moon. Christ, I'm a dork.

I follow Renée inside. There's not much in here. A skylight illuminates some sort of grate, probably an airconditioning unit underneath it. There's a flight of stairs leading down one story. Renée tests the door, but it's locked. Probably just as well; there's likely someone working on the other side of the door, and we don't have an excuse for party-crashing U.N. security.

We head back outside, back to our chosen flagpole. It's time to raise the flag. I grab hold of the rope, tugging it to make sure it's not locked in place.

"Say," I hiss to Renée, "how am I going to fasten the flag to the rope?"

She goes into her handbag. "Here, try these binder clips." She hands me three of the metal clasps, ripped-off office supplies. They're perfect. "Have you seen that guy?" she asks.

"What? Oh, him." I glance over her shoulder. Kneeling down at the other side of the yellow chain, maybe three yards behind me, is a tourist. He's videotaping us. "Yeah, he's still there."

"Okay," Renée says. "I'm going to watch him. I'll tell you when it's safe to go ahead." She takes out her compact and pretends to powder her face, actually watching the tourist in the little mirror.

I signal to Josh to be ready. Bleach is standing off to the side, looking out for the guards. One look at him, at that moment, snaps me out of my doubts. Here is no traitor, no subversive, but a Hero of the Jinx Project: the most highly decorated, the most loyal, and the most valuable field agent ever to serve our struggle.

I have the flag fastened to the rope and ready to hoist. How inconspicuous can you look, standing in the rhododendrons behind a fence, six inches from the sidewalk and its passersby, holding a black flag with a yellow danger symbol, wearing your suit and sunglasses in the full light of a summer afternoon?

"Okay." Renée taps my shoulder. The tourist has left to film some other oddity. It's time.

THE FACE OF NEW YORK

New York has always been the face our country showed the world: the first port of call for millions of immigrants, the capital city for President Washington's inauguration, America's chief destination for visitors from every part of the globe. In the mid–twentieth century, as the United States accepted its role of leadership among nations, it was natural that the United Nations should build its Secretariat here.

It is an honor. The United States recognizes this organization's importance by supporting it with vastly more treasure than any other nation, more than $10 billion per year. On a few occasions, such as the signing of the Universal Declaration of Human Rights, such as the coalitions against North Korea and against Iraq in the 1990s, such as the founding of UNICEF, the United Nations has lived up to the world's confidence in it.

As I hoist the Jinx flag, I think of the U.N.'s abuses: supporting dictatorships in the name of anti-imperialism, condoning Soviet and Chinese communism, and an endless string of anti-Semitic resolutions. These abuses are condemned by the Jinx Project, as by free men and women everywhere. That's why we hang the flag. But I look forward to a wiser future for the

United Nations, as a forum for discussion and debate, embracing a modest role as advisor, eschewing the pretense of sovereignty, encouraging universal liberty and democracy.

The flag reaches the top of the pole. I look down at Josh. He's snapping away. I'm sure he got it. Behind him, Mike stands at salute.

EIGHT TAMMANY'S SHAME:
THE TWEED COURTHOUSE

Mission	TWEED COURTHOUSE, AUGUST 2001
Location	CITY HALL PARK, LOWER MANHATTAN
Goal	ACCESS THE ROOF OF THE INFAMOUS TWEED COURTHOUSE
Officers	LEFTY LEIBOWITZ, L. B. DEYO
Team	BRAZEN, DUNCAN

Attach label, or print or type

REPORTED BY ▼

Lefty Leibowitz

Lefty

I seen my opportunities and I took 'em.

> George Washington Plunkitt,
> *Plunkitt of Tammany Hall* by
> William Riordan, 1905

THE FRUITS OF CORRUPTION

The city's proudest landmarks are tributes to human endeavor directed toward the higher good. The Croton Aqueduct brought fresh, clear water to millions of city inhabitants. Roebling's Brooklyn Bridge was a work of architectural genius that joined two great cities together in perpetuity. Tonight, we will infiltrate New York's most degraded historical monument, a place where corruption and graft reigned supreme.

We meet in City Hall Park, located in lower Manhattan at Broadway between Chambers and Barclay Streets. Brazen, Steve Duncan, L.B., and I wear suits and sunglasses. Steve, as always, is stunning in an all-black ensemble of shirt, tie, and jacket, accompanied by huge sunglasses that cover up half his face. Brazen is slightly more ruffled. He's here to further his research in fractal geometry and to prove a correlation between fractal usage and aesthetic beauty. L.B. and I are wearing our standard outfits, ready for duty.

Named after the seat of the municipal government that stands on its grounds, City Hall Park has always played a key role in the development of the city. Throughout the 1700s, the park was the village green, where criminals received their punishments via public whippings. In 1776, George Washington gathered his troops on the park's grounds and had the Declaration of Independence read to them.

The park is meticulously cared for, with manicured lawns and brilliantly colored flowerbeds lending the setting an idyllic beauty. Two major buildings reside in the park's confines. The first, naturally, is City Hall, where the mayor and the city government perform their day-to-day duties. The second building is the New York County Courthouse, more infamously known as the Tweed Courthouse.

BOSS TWEED

Throughout the 1860s, a man who was not mayor, not an elected official of any kind, ran New York City. William M. Tweed, popularly known as Boss Tweed, was the head of New York's Democratic Party machine, also known as Tammany Hall (named after the party's headquarters on 14th Street). An elaborate system of graft, bribes, and kickbacks kept Boss Tweed and Tammany Hall in control of the city.

Though this era of city politics is renowned for its corruption, the episode that most directly demonstrates its depravity is the construction of the building we are here to see: the New York County Courthouse, begun in 1861 and finished in 1880.

Over the course of this period, the city spent almost $13 million, roughly the equivalent of $231 million today. This was exponentially more expensive than the building should have cost, but the construction was rife with corruption and bribery, and most of the $13 million ended up lining the pockets of Tweed and his cronies. The courthouse cost about twice as much as the purchase of Alaska in 1867. It was a gouging of epic proportions.

When the *New York Times* uncovered the full extent of

the corruption in 1871, citizens were flabbergasted by its depth and reach. One Tammany crony, a plasterer by trade, received payment of $133,187 for two days' work. This was the equivalent of $2.4 million in today's money, and he soon became known as "The Prince of Plasterers." A carpenter who worked for a month got $360,751, or $6.5 million in today's money. The furniture contractor, who supplied the building with three tables and forty chairs, got $179,729 ($3.2 million today).

In addition to the overpayment for labor, government contracts were awarded to companies that Tweed and his associates owned or had direct interest in. Tweed was a partial owner of the quarry that provided the marble for the building. He also owned the printing company that issued the report on why the building was taking so long to complete. The price of the report: an astounding $137,000 in today's money.

After the *Times* printed its exposé on Tweed, he and his associates had to face criminal charges, and many of them ended up in prison. Tweed himself died in jail in 1878, two years before the building was even complete.

THE EXPLORATION BEGINS

It is now several hours past sunset, and the City Hall Park complex is lit only by the street lamps and spotlights that illuminate the two buildings' façades. It is quiet, and as I crane my neck to survey the surroundings I see only a few pedestrians. To my dismay, two police officers stand by the entrance of the train station to our east.

We begin to walk around the perimeter of the Tweed Courthouse, looking for a point of entry. Its gorgeous white walls shine in the moonlight. It is a brick building with granite cladding, with two wings joined in the center by a third main section. The north wing is designed in an Anglo-Italianate style. It is reminiscent of the palaces of Renaissance Europe, as filtered through the eyes of the British gentlemen's clubs of the 1800s. The southern wing is designed in a Romanesque style, and also features an ornate rotunda with a domed stained-glass roof. A Corinthian portico graces the center section, adding further to the aura of sophistication.

Most of the building is surrounded by a wooden fence, evidently put up by the construction workers who have worked at the site for the last several years. At the time of our adventure, there are plans to turn the courthouse into the new location for the Museum of the City of New York (though, as it turned out, it would ultimately come to house the Board of Education). Renovations are under way to restore the building to its original glory. The building hasn't been used as a courthouse since the 1920s, and age has taken its toll. The wooden fence is to prevent gawkers and pedestrians from straying too close to the workers and to keep out unwanted guests. Within a short time, it seems, the Tweed Courthouse will again be open to the public as the site of such exhibitions as "The Stick Ball Hall of Fame" and "A Treasury of New York City Silver." Tonight it is open only to the corrupt ghosts of Boss Tweed and his cronies, and us.

We begin our perimeter walk on the south side of the building. Here, the wooden fence has a few two- to three-inch breaks where adjacent panels butt up to one another—not nearly wide enough for a person to slip through, but certainly wide enough for a peek at the courthouse.

I press my face against a break in the fence and peer inside. The courthouse lies about twenty feet back, a swath of dirt separating the granite of the building from where we stand. There is a doorway built into the building at about the midway point. The door is wide open.

We turn the corner toward the east side of the building. On this side there is no fence—just a large grass field that fronts City Hall Park. Construction debris is everywhere: tarps, dust, odd machines, buckets. An open window on the ground floor leads to an ornate central room.

On the north side of the building is its official entrance. A single security guard is at the gate, sitting in a chair and looking bored. The guard stiffens up and eyes us. He clutches a walkie-talkie that is attached to the loop in his belt. We keep moving.

The west side is barricaded by a huge, impenetrable fence and provides little hope of access, so we decide to enter the building where there is no fence, and then make our way back along the courthouse perimeter. There, safely hidden in the darkness, we can enter through one of the doorways. A couple walking through the park slow their pace to stare at us suspiciously as they pass.

The four of us move into position and dart, one by one, over the grass and behind the fence. Gaining initial access is always the scariest part of an expedition. Anyone who is nearby now could see us in the act of trespassing. We move as quickly as we can. No more than ten seconds pass, and we are again out of view. We walk back toward the open doorway, the fence on our left and the courthouse on our right. I look up at the building's monstrous windows, but I can't make out what's inside. Things have gone amazingly well so far. We are less than one hundred yards from City Hall, and the security here should be stringent. So far, this has been way too easy.

Another fifty feet, and we pass though the main doorway. We have entered the Tweed Courthouse, the shame and the pride of the city.

IN THE COURTHOUSE

The entranceway to the courthouse is dark, though enough light enters the vestibule from secondary sources to allow us to make our way without bumping into any walls. A staircase leads up to our right, which we quickly climb. Once on the second floor, we are given the choice to continue upward on the staircase or to walk through a doorway to our left that opens up into one of the courthouse side rooms. We choose the latter.

The room is a good introduction to the courthouse: It is majestic, even in its current state of disrepair. The ceilings are at least twenty-five feet high, and the walls are adorned with gold inlays and detail work. It is cavernous, approximately one thousand square feet. The five of us wander from one side to the other and stare out the huge windows that open out toward the adjacent City Hall, just one hundred yards or so to our south.

Our journeys over the last few months have taken us to the most remote places in our city: the deserted Smallpox Hospital; the dark underworld of the Freedom Tunnel. Now we are just a stone's throw from where most of the monumental decisions in the history of New York have been made. The 108 mayors of the city worked at their desks across the lawn from us and, for better or for worse, made their marks. Men from the first one hundred years of New York's life as a city in the newly formed United States of America, like Richard Varick and DeWitt Clinton, are mostly remembered as the namesakes of downtown streets. After Greater New York was formed in 1898 (whereby the city incorporated

Brooklyn, Queens, the Bronx, and Staten Island), other names joined the list. Here are a few of them:

- Robert Van Wyck (mayor from 1898–1901), beset by corruption charges, sneaked out the back door of City Hall on his successor's inauguration day and blended into the crowd to avoid being recognized
- George B. McClellan (1904–1909) oversaw the construction of the Queensboro and Manhattan Bridges, the Municipal Building, and the Catskill water system
- John Purroy Mitchel (1914–1917), the thirty-five-year-old "Boy Mayor," was the first to create a comprehensive city budget
- Jimmy Walker (1926–1932), the nightclubbing "Beau James," caroused with movie stars and actresses and resigned amidst yet another corruption scandal
- Fiorello LaGuardia (1934–1945), the "Little Flower," became one of the city's most beloved mayors by restoring the public's faith in city government
- Robert F. Wagner (1954–1965) began or completed such projects as the Van Wyck Expressway, the Grand Central Parkway, the Long Island Expressway, the Verrazano-Narrows and Throgs Neck Bridges, Shea Stadium, and Lincoln Center for the Performing Arts
- Abe Beame (1974–1977) failed to secure federal funding for the bankrupt city and inspired the *Daily News* headline FORD TO CITY: DROP DEAD

These stewards for this metropolis have overseen the construction of all of the places we've explored this summer. Would they appreciate what we're doing here tonight? They sure weren't above winking at the rules now and again. But the entire apparatus of the city's security is in place to prevent us from reaching our goal. Will we be able to conquer the roof of the Tweed Courthouse?

Steve leads the way, stealthily moving up the second flight of stairs to the third floor. The building is empty and silent. Any sound we make echoes throughout the massive interior. We keep our communications to a whisper and tread softly across the polished floors. As we walk, we're careful to hide in the shadows and to keep away from the windows that expose us to the outside world.

The fear inherent in this expedition is not of getting killed, but of getting caught. We are in a building that is mostly well lit. It is alarmed and protected by electronic surveillance devices. There's an active security guard on duty. Cops and pedestrians surround us in the park outside. Any one of them could see us through the windows of the courthouse and report their suspicions. Our footsteps and our whispers are amplified in the empty halls. I'm sure we'll be heard. Making it through the whole summer without getting arrested is too much to ask for.

Once on the third floor, we move off the narrow service staircase and head toward the center of the building. The main hallways of the courthouse are particularly bright, so we'll have to be extra cautious. We turn to the north and enter the main part of the building. A huge staircase stands to our left, approximately twenty feet wide and accompanied by impressively carved handrails. A film of fine dust is sprinkled across the floor, much of it already imprinted with the treads of our shoes. To our right is the huge domed rotunda that was responsible for almost a third of the cost of construction. The dome is decorated with a stained-glass ceiling that filters in the moonlight of this warm night.

Steve Duncan pulls a small black digital camera out of his bag and begins snapping pictures. I stand to the side, my back pressed against the wall, looking up and admiring the exquisite dome above our heads.

Brazen and L.B. have crossed to the other side of the rotunda, where the southern wing of the building resides. They silently wave Steve and me over. We tiptoe to join them.

This side of the building has several more huge side rooms, similar to the one we had seen downstairs, all audaciously ornate and empty save for the refurbishing equipment being used by the workers.

Not everyone has been able to see past the courthouse's scandalous taint. "The whole atmosphere is corrupt," said an anonymous reformer who fought Tammany Hall. "You look up at its ceilings and find gaudy decorations; you wonder which is the greatest, the vulgarity or the corruptness of the place."

We head up another staircase, hoping to find our way to the roof and the stained-glass dome. We soon find ourselves in the building's maintenance area, a huge section filled with pipes and ventilation equipment. The smell of the insulation materials is strong as we continue forward up a final staircase, a narrow set of metal steps that lacks any of the glamour of the others we've climbed tonight.

At the top of the stairs a doorway opens up onto the roof. Brazen and Steve step out first, followed by L.B. and myself. The roof is pitched to a slight angle, easy enough to walk on but still warranting caution. We are about halfway down its southern half. A few steeple-like structures dot the roof—they seem to be alternate entranceways to the roof that emanate from the floors below. Amidst these, at the roof's highest point, is another midsize structure with a doorway on the south end. I climb toward it, carefully planting each step firmly on the roof as I move. We're extremely exposed to public view here. Any of the pedestrians in the park below would see us if he simply looked up. I glance over my shoulder as I walk to see if we've been spotted. I see nothing.

The roof affords quite a view of lower Manhattan and Brooklyn. We're across the street from the Brooklyn Bridge, now aglow with its nighttime lights, as well as the lights of the cars that travel between the two great boroughs. Across the East River, I can see the buildings of downtown Brooklyn and the countless homes that stretch off into the distance toward Long Island. Before the incorporation of Brooklyn into greater New York, it was its own city, one that rivaled Manhattan in size and scope. Even today, Brooklyn, if an independent city, would be the fifth largest in the United States.

To our south, the Twin Towers of the World Trade Center are approximately a half-mile away, standing guard over the city's financial district as they have every night for the last twenty-eight years. They are the tallest buildings in New York City, and, at one time, in the world. We've heard that occasionally maintenance workers are hired to repair the giant antenna that sprouts from one of the towers. We want to climb that antenna and plant the Jinx flag at the highest point. We've already called friends in the press who might gain access for us.

I continue the climb to the structure at the roof's apex and am the last to arrive. L.B. and Brazen wait outside, peering into its windows. Steve has already begun climbing through.

This is where they maintain the stained-glass roof over the Rotunda, Brazen tells me, and as I look into the window I can see the same brightly colored glass that we had been staring up at just a few minutes before. A small catwalk runs around the perimeter of the floor, the center of which is made up of the stained glass itself. A network of ladderlike ceiling beams spread evenly across its roof.

A reformer said that the courthouse "was conceived in sin, and its dome, if ever finished, will be glazed all over with iniquity." As far as Steve is concerned, the only thing the dome is glazed with is opportunity for reckless endangerment. He is already inside the structure, hanging over the stained glass by one of the ceiling beams. His feet dangle in midair about five feet above the glass. He swings from beam to beam as if they were monkey bars. If he lets go, or loses his grip, he will crash through the glass and fall four stories to the ground floor below.

As for me, I take out my pocket tape recorder and record the details of our conquest in a hushed voice.

THE LEGACY OF THE COURTHOUSE

Ironically, the events in the aftermath of the corruption at the Tweed Courthouse led to direct improvements in the lives of New Yorkers. Tammany Hall's patronage system was dismantled after the cries for reform became deafening. Slowly, the influence of the political bosses began to wane. New civil service laws were passed, which caused government jobs to be awarded on the basis of an applicant's merit, rather than as a reward for cronyism and connections. The lower- and working-class immigrants who had made up much of Tammany's constituency and membership also began to make advances via other avenues. Eventually, the building which last housed Tammany was sold and is now the New York Film Academy, located at Union Square. The name and symbol of Tammany Hall can still be seen above the Academy's doorway.

Though the Tweed Courthouse is in some ways a symbol of the dark side of New York City and its political system, it's also a throwback to a romantic era when every mayor had a nickname, and when fat guys with big cigars and lots of gold jewelry ran the show from shadowy headquarters in the seediest of districts. At Jinx, we've certainly been inspired by Boss Tweed in our ambitions to ruthlessly control the city with underhanded tactics and devious schemes. Soon we'll establish our own machine in our Chinatown office. There we can draft our plans for the construction of a Jinx Courthouse for the propagation of urban adventure.

NINE

THE ATHENAEUM ⚠

Mission	
THE ATHENAEUM SOCIETY	
Location	
THE GERSHWIN HOTEL, MANHATTAN	
Goal	
TO MEET WITH THE UE COMMUNITY AND DISCUSS INTELLIGENCE AND GOALS	
Officers	
LEFTY LEIBOWITZ, L. B. DEYO	
Team	
SPEED LEVITCH, JULIA DARK PASSAGE, NINJALICIOUS, SOCIETY ORIENTALIST BRETT X, THE PROFESSOR, DR. NO-NO, STEFAN JACKSON, BRAIN EVANCHIK, AGENT BLEACH, GABRIEL ARIELLE	

Attach label, or print or type

REPORTED BY ▼

Lefty Leibowitz

Lefty

Then Ulysses of many wiles answered her, and said:
Hard is it, Goddess, for a mortal man to know you
when he meets you, how wise to any extent he be, for
you take what shape you will.

But this I know well, that of old you were kindly
toward me, so long as we sons of the Achaeans were
warring in the land of Troy.

Homer, *The Odyssey*

THE BEGINNINGS OF THE CULTURE OF ADVENTURE

At the dawn of Western civilization, men of wisdom gathered in Athens to discuss and to debate the latest philosophical and scientific issues. Plato and Aristotle took their cues from the goddess Athena, who reigned on Olympus as the queen of wisdom and the arts, as well as war. She was said to have bequeathed to the Greeks such inventions as the plow, the flute, shipbuilding, shoemaking, and the taming of animals. Wearing a breastplate decorated with the head of the Gorgon Medusa and carrying her fearsome shield and thunderbolt, Athena was a symbol of the power and glory of ancient Athens and its culture. The great thinkers of the day tried to emulate her model by contributing their own ideas to the advancement of Greek civilization. In the open squares of the city they would read their most recent treatises, critique any logical faults in the works of others, and use the Socratic method in the free exchange of ideas.

In the second century A.D., the Greeks were conquered by the Romans, and this practice of public oratory, thought, and debate became institutionalized by one of the greatest of the early Roman emperors. Hadrian (117–138) was a lover of Greek culture and philosophy, and when he founded a proto-university in 135, he dedicated it to Athena and the Greek tradition that had come before him. He called it the Athenaeum.

The Roman scholars of the Athenaeum plied their trade for a few hundred more years, living off imperial largesse so that they might pursue their philosophical goals with full attention. Soon the ever-increasing tide of barbarian hordes to the north began to overrun imperial Rome's institutions, and eventually Hadrian's Athenaeum was no more.

With Europe plunged into the Dark Ages, it wasn't until the cultural boom of the Renaissance that the ideals of the Athenaeum began to attract once more the attention of the West's brightest minds. With the pursuit of secular enlightenment again a priority, Athenaeums became active as temples of free thought, where any manner of hypothesis could be explored without fear of persecution. A famous Renaissance view of the Athenaeum can be seen in Raphael's *The School of Athens*, a painting featuring Plato and Aristotle at the height of their philosophical powers.

The admiration of the Athenaeum continued to grow in western Europe, until it reached its culmination in the creation of London's Athenaeum Club in 1824. The club, dedicated to the literary, scientific, and artistic attainments of its members, quickly became one of the most famous men's clubs in London, regularly attended by such intellectual luminaries as Sir Richard Francis Burton and Oscar Wilde.

JINX, COMMUNITY, AND THE
MODERN-DAY ATHENAEUM

All of this now seems mere prelude to the Jinx Athenaeum Society, founded by L.B. and myself in 1999 and dedicated, as in the case of Hadrian's Athenaeum, to the goals of secular enlightenment and learning. By this time we had been writing about urban exploration in *Jinx* magazine for almost two years, and we wanted to create a place where fellow explorers could gather to discuss their latest adventures, discoveries, and thoughts. Our hope was twofold: first, that by treating the fruits of urban exploration in a scientific way, as empirical data to be shared with fellow travelers and the public at large, we could demonstrate the intrinsic value of our work. Second, we wanted to build on an already burgeoning sense of community in the urban exploration world and share in the excitement of building friendships with others who share our eccentric worldview.

Of course I always knew that there were other people who took an interest in exploring the city. It wasn't until I met an unusual character named Ninjalicious, however, that I began to get an idea of the scope of the UE community around the world.

Shortly after the release of *Jinx* #3 (our first real attempt to share our ideas about urban exploration with the public), I received a thick envelope in the mail postmarked Toronto, Canada. I opened the envelope and inside found a handwritten note and several copies of a photocopied pamphlet entitled *Infiltration: The Zine About Going Places You're Not Supposed to Go.*

The note was straightforward and to the point. It

explained how the writer (the aforementioned "Ninjalicious") had discovered a copy of our magazine in a local Toronto store. He had been intrigued by one article in particular, entitled "Urban Mountaineering," that told the story of our climb to the pinnacle of the Broadway Bridge that connects northern Manhattan and the Bronx. The mysterious Ninja, it turned out, had his own publication in which he felt we might be interested.

Accompanying the note in the envelope were three copies of his pamphlet. I picked up the first, apparently on the topic of Toronto hotels, and began to read:

THE BASICS OF HOTEL EXPLORATION

Exploring hotels requires a mix of stealth and social engineering. Unless one sticks strictly to the unused areas of a hotel, there will be many times when one must interact with other people, including employees.

Hotel employees are a lot like bears: though they'll certainly attack you if you act scared or run from them, under normal circumstances they would really prefer to avoid a confrontation altogether. They know all too well that any sort of conflict with a hotel guest could result in serious punishment, so they're as scared of you as you are of them.

After a few more paragraphs of introduction and a nice photograph of a young man cavorting in a luxurious swimming pool, I hit the heart of the issue: a comprehensive study of the recreational facilities of nearly twenty hotels in the Toronto metropolitan area, beginning with the two-star hotels and incrementally working its way toward the five-star hotels. Each listing was an exhaustive study of the particular hotel with tips and advice on how the intrepid explorer might best access the swimming pool, gym, and sauna. Maps were included, along with a key that showed the location of potential hazards, like security guards, locked doors, and cameras. Specific strategies for gaining access and avoiding suspicion were covered, for example switching into a bathing suit in one of the hotel maintenance closets before hitting the pool or carrying around a notebook and cell phone in order to feign legitimacy. Most articles were accompanied by photos of our hero swimming blissfully in his most recent conquest, security assuredly oblivious to his success.

I was immediately charmed by the finesse and intelligence of this young ninja. I was delighted that someone had gone to such trouble, and engaged in such nefarious methods, to satisfy his curiosity in a nonmalevolent way. I wrote back to Ninjalicious to thank him for the pamphlets (the other two issues dealt with topics like the Paris catacombs and the Scottish rail tunnels) and also asked if I could interview him for the next issue of *Jinx*.

Our conversation lasted well over an hour. I learned that the Ninj was in his early twenties and had lived in Canada for his whole life, and that he had begun his urban explorations when one night, suffering from insomnia, he infiltrated the historic Victoria Hospital in downtown Toronto. I learned of his travels to the subway tunnels and dockyards of the city. But I was most intrigued to find out that he had started a Web-based discussion group for fellow urban explorers, and that people from around the world had joined and regularly discussed their adventures. Ninja happily informed me that he would be placing my e-mail address on the list and that I would begin receiving notices from the group immediately.

That night I checked my e-mail and found six messages on the topic of "The Ethics of Lockpicking." Six different people, from several different countries, had chimed in with their opinions. Immediately, the wheels in my head started turning. If the Ninja's online community had been so successful, imagine what might happen if someone could create a community of urban explorers that met in person. It was the answer to a question L.B. and I had been wrestling with for months: We wanted to create a social experience centered on *Jinx* magazine, but we didn't know exactly what it should be. We just knew we didn't want it to devolve into another boring party, centered on nothing but music and alcohol. Somehow, we knew we had to incorporate *Jinx*'s mission, promoting worldwide urban adventure, into the experience.

Thus, the Jinx Athenaeum Society was born one evening late in 1999. Every month we would arrange a unique program, featuring a series of discussions, presentations, and debates of interest to the forty to sixty meeting attendees. Over the next two years we would stage debates with topics like: "Resolved: Communism is still a threat." And "Resolved: Birkenstocks should be banned." Our Society Orientalist, Brett X, would lecture us on the history of Tamerlane, the great Mongol warlord. Brain Evanchik would enlighten the attendees with his thoughts on game theory and mutual assured destruction.

A TRIP TO THE JINX ATHENAEUM SOCIETY

The Gershwin Hotel is tucked away on a side street in midtown Manhattan, a gaudy and colorful speck in a sea of nondescript office buildings. The façade and interior of the hotel are decorated with Pop Art by luminaries such as Andy Warhol and Roy Lichtenstein. It is here that on the first Wednesday of every month urban explorers from all over the world come to socialize and share tales of their adventures.

This particular Wednesday, the midsize room where the monthly meetings are held is packed with upward of fifty attendees. As is my usual habit before the beginning of society meetings, I am pacing the floor in my blue argyle sweater vest, stopping every few moments to look at my watch. As moderator of tonight's meeting, my first duty is to begin in a punctual manner so as not to encourage tardiness in the future.

There will be two events tonight: Our Medal of Honor winner Agent Bleach will do a short presentation on "The Art of Disguise," after which a debate will be held between L.B. and Brain Evanchik on the topic "Resolved: The Age of Discovery is not dead: It lives on through urban explorers." Afterward, the entire group will retire to the hotel bar, where further conversation will likely continue into the early morning.

It is now 7:55, and there are only five minutes remaining before the commencement of the evening's entertainment. Already, the room looks like an all-star gathering of New York's urban exploration elite. In the far right corner I notice the one and only Agent Bleach sitting quietly and reviewing his notes. He wears a black suit, a brilliant red fez, and an opulent gold medal. The medal and fez were given to him as honors by the most senior officers of the Jinx Project, in a ceremony that has never been duplicated. About six months prior to this meeting, Agent Bleach had been awarded the highly coveted Jinx Medal of Honor, as mentioned earlier. The Medal of Honor (and accompanying fez) had been awarded to Agent Bleach for his bravery in the line of duty during the crafting of a report he authored for *Jinx* #4 titled

"Deep Underground: A 24-Hour Subway Odyssey." In it, Bleach told of his twenty-four-hour adventure in the New York City subway system, during which he traveled on every line and through every borough, never leaving the confines of the system. An excerpt for your edification:

> Leaving the death-tainted shuttle train to board the Queens-bound A train in a notoriously unsafe Brooklyn neighborhood, I scan the faces of its many passengers to read impending, violent death—possibly mine. As I note the nearest door and emergency brake, a man enters my car wearing a "horse" around his waist, with jeans and attached shoes dangling from both sides to represent his legs. The Horseman of the A train bucks wildly, striking his mount with a stick and punctuating his ride with a rhythmic chant of "Mm Mm-mm, Fuckin Mm-mm, Mm Mm-mm, Fuckin Mm-mm." This diversion is enough to ensure my safe passage.

Bleach, to his credit, has been an extremely proud recipient of the honor conferred upon him by Jinx and is always seen in full regalia at Athenaeum Society meetings.

A few feet to Bleach's right, looking resplendent in a black, knee-length skirt, is the young Miss Arielle, a longtime associate of ours who also happens to be director of publicity at the Counter Spy Shop, a world-renowned store that specializes in providing government employees and corporate clients with the latest in high-tech surveillance and espionage equipment. I walk over to greet her, and as I do, I thank her for her presentation from the month before, when she was kind enough to bring in several of her company's gadgets for our perusal. With the polished confidence of an expert saleswoman, she demonstrated each of the products she had brought for us that evening: a GPS tracking device that could be placed beneath a car in order to survey its location; tiny cameras hidden inside a teddy bear's eyes; a booby-trapped briefcase that sends a debilitating shock through anyone who dares to pick it up; and a wide range of night-vision glasses and goggles. Though most of the equipment was expensive and beyond the meager means of the Athenaeum Society attendees, the mere thought of being able to use this equipment quickened our collective pulses.

After speaking briefly with Arielle, I turn to head back toward the podium at the front of the room. It's time to begin the event. As I walk, I am happy to see so many familiar faces: Julia, whose exploration group Dark Passage first gained notoriety for serving a full four-course meal to guests in formal wear on an abandoned set of tracks in a Brooklyn subway tunnel. Since then she has gone on to become, along with Toronto's Ninjalicious, one of the most respected and intrepid of all the explorers. Space Commander Stefan, so-named because of his position as head of Jinx's space program, glowers menacingly behind a pair of dark sunglasses, perhaps still angry that some of the more foolish Society members failed to take his presentation from two months ago, "Why Jinx Must Win the Space Race," as seriously as he had hoped. Marcy "The Professor" Shoemaker, sitting two seats to his right, flips slowly through a stack of photographs from her most recent trip to Havana, where she had gathered useful intelligence on Cuba's Communist government. Dr. No-No, a graduate student at Columbia's epidemiology program, goes over data from her latest study on the spread of disease through New York's slums.

After taking the final few steps to the stage, I pick up

the microphone that is provided to us by the hotel staff and turn it on. "Testing, testing. One . . . two . . . three," I say. I can't quite tell if the amplifier in the back of the room is working or not.

"What are you trying to do, blow our eardrums out?" Marcy yells back. Her role as expert in Cuban culture is augmented by her role as the Athenaeum Society's preeminent heckler. More than a few speakers have been on the receiving end of her caustic commentary and questioning.

"Hello, everyone. Welcome to this month's meeting of the Jinx Athenaeum Society. My name is Lefty Leibowitz, and I will be your host for the evening. If anyone would like a copy of *Jinx* magazine or this evening's program, please see Agent Gabriel in the back."

A few people reach out for a copy of the program, which features a list of the evening's events. It also boasts a portrait of Arctic explorer Ernest Shackleton and a list of the Athenaeum Society virtues: invention, arrangement, diction, action, and memory, as well as danger, adventure, and the underground.

"Tonight we've got a very special evening planned for you," I continue. "We'll be starting off with a presentation from our very own Medal of Honor winner, Mr. Agent Bleach, titled 'The Art of Disguise.' Afterward, in the grand tradition of Athenaeum's past, we will have a debate on the topic 'Resolved: The Age of Discovery is not dead: It lives on through urban explorers.' Arguing against the resolution will be Society President L. B. Deyo. Arguing for will be Brain Evanchik. Now, with no further ado, let's get Agent Bleach up here for his presentation on 'The Art of Disguise.'"

As I finish my introduction, my eyes scan the room for Agent Bleach, but he is nowhere to be found. There is no sign of the deep and brilliant scarlet of the Jinx fez or the golden gleam of his esteemed medal. A few moments of awkward silence pass. An older man, hunched over and carrying a cane, glasses perched on a bulbous red nose, rises from his chair and pulls his tan English hunting cap over his graying head.

As a few more seconds pass, I become increasingly nervous about Agent Bleach's whereabouts. As the old man starts to walk from the back of the room towards the front exit, I realize that if Bleach doesn't show up soon, we could begin to lose our guests.

Suddenly, the old man, who is now by the front of the stage, stops and looks at me with an amused smile. I stare back, bewildered by his bizarre behavior. He reaches out his hand for the microphone, and in a moment everything becomes clear. Beneath the wrinkled folds of skin I see the unmistakable jawline and bright, flashing eyes of our very own Medal of Honor winner, Agent Bleach.

I hand Bleach the microphone, and as he steps on the stage he takes off his hat, glasses, and prosthetic nose, revealing himself to the audience.

"Greetings, ladies and gentleman," he begins. "I have come here to speak with you all tonight about one of the most important elements in urban exploration, the art of disguise. As you all know, in many cases it is quite difficult to access a particular locale for exploration, and we have to use whatever tools we have available to grasp victory from the jaws of defeat. Last month, we learned about the art of surveillance from Arielle, but I believe that the element of disguise, whether utilized to hide one's identity or to act as a credibility aid, is just as important in operating a successful mission."

Bleach turns away from the audience and picks up a long metal pointer. He also uncovers an easel on the stage that had been covered with a white cloth. On the easel sits a series of large white placards. The uppermost is inscribed with a delicate script reading "The Art of Disguise: A Presentation by Jinx Medal of Honor winner Agent Bleach."

Bleach removes the uppermost placard and places it on the ground, revealing beneath it a large photograph of himself cavorting at a nightclub, his eyes obscured by a pair of dark sunglasses, his hair hidden beneath a bright silver wig. He wears black lipstick and a form-fitting leather shirt.

"The most important aspects of a disguise are the eyes and head," Bleach explains. "When the eyes and head are hidden, the most identifiable features can no longer be used by others as a means to uncover your disguise. It's precisely the tactic I used one evening at our local nightclub, and I managed to go the whole night without being recognized by my ex-girlfriend."

As Bleach talks, I think of another man who relied on his disguise to help him find his way through an even more precarious predicament than Bleach's.

In 1855, Captain Sir Richard Francis Burton was one of the first westerners to penetrate the forbidden Muslim holy cities of Mecca and Medina. To sneak in, Burton elaborately disguised himself as an Arab hajj, or pilgrim. He wore the traditional dress of the Arabian Peninsula and traveled with a large entourage of Arab servants and guides. In his Arab-style turban, he scrupulously followed the first part of Bleach's advice. Without Jinx-issue sunglasses, however, he was forced to risk his expedition with eyes exposed.

It is for this adventure and others that we consider Burton to be the consummate Jinx adventurer, even profiling him in *Jinx* #3. In some ways he laid the foundation for our modern-day urban exploration by probing already inhabited and mapped cities for their unknown histories and culture. Over the course of his life, he accomplished feat after feat of breathtaking bravery and intelligence. In addition to his voyages to the great Muslim holy cities, he was the first to translate such works as the *Kama Sutra, The Arabian Nights,* and *The Perfumed Garden.* Along with John Hanning Speke, he discovered Lake Tanganyika and played a pivotal role in the discovery of the source of the Nile. He spoke twenty-seven languages, along with varying dialects of many of them. He dabbled in other religions, a practice viewed with horror by most of his Victorian contemporaries. He went so far as to receive the holy brahminical thread from his Hindu guru, as well as to engage in Sufi rites with a congregation of whirling dervishes in Sind. He was known to have a voracious sexual appetite, often chronicling in his journals the various sexual practices of the prostitutes around the world whose company he enjoyed.

THE DEBATE

By this time, Agent Bleach has made quite a bit of progress with his presentation. He has gone through the majority of his placards, each having featured a photograph of Bleach in a different disguise, many in the tradition of his vampire race. Along the way he has given much advice of practical use to the urban explorers in the crowd. Finally, Bleach stops and asks the audience if there are any questions before he concludes.

A lone hand shoots up in the air. It belongs to one Timothy "Speed" Levitch, currently the Athenaeum Society's Poet Laureate. Over the last few years he has gained a certain level of fame from his performance in an independent film called *The Cruise,* which chronicled his life as a tour bus guide in New York City. Agent Bleach points to Speed, who begins to speak.

"I just want to say that your presentation has been an effervescent homage to the present tense." Speed is known for his poetic use of gibberish, and he has outdone himself again with his inscrutable praise of Bleach's work.

Agent Bleach scratches his head, confused. As the audience breaks into spontaneous applause, I bound back onto the stage and take the microphone.

"Thank you, Agent Bleach! Let's give our Medal of Honor winner a big hand." The applause continues.

Agent Bleach steps off the stage and heads back to his chair. Along the way he is the recipient of many pats on the back and high fives.

I clutch the microphone and my face takes on a serious look. "Ladies and gentlemen, fellow Jinx agents, urban explorers. It is now time for the main event of the evening: a debate on a topic that is close to everyone's heart. Resolved: The Age of Discovery is not dead: It lives on through the urban explorers. We've got two fine panelists here tonight to debate this proposed resolution. First, let me introduce a man who is working on his philosophy thesis at the University of Texas, a man who fights for truth and justice: Brain Evanchik!"

Brain rises from his chair and takes his place on the

stage. He is wearing a full beard, in the style of Rasputin, and is dressed in a sweater and sports jacket. He looks as if he has just stepped off the University of Texas campus, where his professors have anxiously been awaiting his missing thesis for the last four years.

"Second," I continue, "I'd like to introduce a man that most of you are familiar with. He is the director of the Jinx Project and the president of the Jinx Athenaeum Society. Let's give him a big hand: L. B. Deyo!"

L.B. strides to the front of the room amidst a smattering of clapping and boos. In his dark suit and with eyes always impenetrable and covered by dark shades, he is known for debating with absolute and unswerving conviction, often taking a quasi-fascist style of oratory, complete with dramatic hand gestures and soaring perorations. For many in the audience, he plays the role of the *bête noir* when on the debating platform. As much as they may be fond of him when off stage, they can't help but join in the fun of rooting against him during the debate and voting against him after it. He has yet to win an Athenaeum Society debate.

I begin to explain the rules. "The format for tonight's debate will be very simple. We will start with the opening statements. Then there will be a series of rebuttals. We will close with final statements. After the final statements, we will have a vote on whether to pass this resolution. Let's begin. L.B., you have the floor."

L.B., a portrait of calm and reserve at this early point in the debate, rises from his chair and begins his introduction. "Urban exploration is a wonderful hobby and a fascinating practice, but it is not comparable to the Golden Age of Exploration that went on during past centuries. During those times, explorers were engaged in discovering places that were completely unknown to the western world. They were unmapped and unheard of. They dealt with cultures that had never seen a European before. That Golden Age of Exploration is now dead. Urban explorers spend their time poking around in cities that are completely mapped, that are completely inhabited, and that are completely known. To call urban exploration a continuation of the Golden Age is to insult those greats like Magellan, Columbus, de Leon, and Cook who risked their lives for the advancement of science and knowledge!"

As L.B. speaks, Brain grows visibly agitated. He is fidgeting in his chair and perspiring profusely as he listens. Every few seconds he runs his hands through his uncombed hair, and after several minutes of this treatment his head resembles a wasps' nest. The overall effect is of a muttering madman, consumed with rage and frustration. He bounds to his feet and practically forces L.B. back to his chair. As he begins to speak, he paces the stage. Every few steps he pauses and glares out at the audience. His face is twisted into a mask of intensity, as if he is gathering up all of his emotional and intellectual energy for the battle to come. Finally, he launches into his own introduction, his voice strained with excitement, his unique take on the New York accent burning the eardrums of the assembled.

"Esteemed colleagues, we've heard from L.B. here a particular point of view about urban exploration and the Age of Exploration. It is a view fraught with cynicism and self-loathing! I would like to present a different view, perhaps one that is more thoughtful and also more optimistic about the value that urban explorers have to the world. It is my contention that urban explorers are indeed a logical extension of the great explorers of the past ages. While it is true that the continents have been mapped in this modern age, it is also true that there is much knowledge of the modern city that has been lost. Our cities have become so complex, so overwrought with layer after layer of complexity, that there is really no one person who understands how all of these layers work together. It is true that New York is an inhabited city, but so was Mexico before Cortez. So was Harare before Burton. The history of exploration is the history of the discovery of inhabited places in which there is information to be gained or uncovered by the explorer. Our modern-day cities are a perfect example of such lost knowledge, and why it is imperative upon us that we urban explorers take the attitude of the classical explorers in our travels. And it is imperative that we gather knowledge and hard empirical facts to share with our communities. That is the only way for knowledge to grow."

Brain exhales a deep sigh and turns back to his chair on the debating stand, a smug smile planted on his face. As he sits, he issues a challenging look to L.B. A small strand of saliva floats from the corner of Brain's mouth.

"Mr. Chairman." L.B. shoots a look in my direction. "This is ridiculous. For Mr. Brain to try to pretend that urban explorers can be compared to the greats of history is insulting to me and to all Americans."

"Please, seat yourself, Mr. Deyo," Brain thunders. "I have much more to say. As an urban explorer, I honor and revere the contributions of the great explorers of the past, but please don't denigrate our own contribution to the archives of adventure. We may not be discovering the world's tallest mountain or most remote island, but we do discover something a little more subtle, something that is a little harder to put into words. And unless you've been on the top of the Brooklyn Bridge, surrounded by death on all sides, it might be a little hard for you to fully grasp."

I stand on the side of the stage, intermittently looking at my watch (so that I can monitor the length of the debate) and the audience, which by now seems fully engaged in the proceedings. I notice our Society Orientalist Brett X whispering excitedly to Agent Bleach, and I wonder on which side of the issue they come down.

L.B. and Brain continue their arguments, and soon it is time for the concluding arguments. I ask them to pause their rebuttals, and once more each takes the stage in an orderly manner, making the case one more time for each side.

When they are finished, I take the microphone and ask the congregants to vote yay or nay on the resolution via a show of hands. The final tally is 26 yay and 25 nay. L.B. has lost another debate.

As the participants leave the stage, I thank the audience for their attendance and their attention. The only item left on the agenda now is the post-meeting celebration in the hotel bar. One by one, the society members gather up their things and move into the adjoining room. They will stay there until the early hours of the morning, discussing and showing photographs of their recent explorations, debating further tonight's resolution, and enjoying a beautiful evening as urban explorers.

The Athenaeum Society is by now an established aspect of the urban exploration community. Month after month we gather together to pool our resources and intelligence, and to uncover more completely that which lies beneath the surface. With the growing complexity of our urban environments, we know that it is only through collaboration and social interaction that we can get a full picture of the city as it truly is. By creating an organization specializing in human intelligence, and expert in a broad variety of subjects, from space administration to Orientalism, from poetry to Communism to aesthetics, we can bring together the various disciplines that have shaped western culture and apply their wisdom to our own practice. With our own sincerity of purpose, coupled with the divine wisdom of Athena, we have helped the history of the Athenaeum to find its great culmination in Jinx. Plato and Aristotle must be grateful.

TEN

FIRE BURN AND CAULDRON BUBBLE:

NORTH BROTHER ISLAND AND HELL GATE

<table>
<tr><td rowspan="6" style="vertical-align:middle">Attach label, or print or type</td></tr>
<tr><td>Mission
RIVERSIDE HOSPITAL, SUMMER 2001</td></tr>
<tr><td>Location
NORTH BROTHER ISLAND, EAST RIVER</td></tr>
<tr><td>Goal
EXPLORE THE HOSPITAL AND GROUNDS</td></tr>
<tr><td>Officers
LEFTY LEIBOWITZ, L. B. DEYO</td></tr>
<tr><td>Team
SPECIAL AGENT RENÉE</td></tr>
</table>

REPORTED BY ▼

L. B. Deyo

L. B. Deyo

And thus too, it happened, that before the last echoes
of the last chime had utterly sunk into silence, there
were many individuals in the crowd who had found
leisure to become aware of the presence of a masked
figure which had arrested the attention of no single
individual before.

> Edgar Allan Poe, "The
> Masque of the Red Death"

> Round about the cauldron go:
> In the poison'd entrails throw.

> Shakespeare, *Macbeth*,
> Act IV, i

THE *GENERAL SLOCUM*

On the morning of June 15, 1904, over thirteen hundred
German-Americans, members of St. Mark's Lutheran
Evangelical Church, boarded a ferry. She was the *General
Slocum*, bound for Huntington, Long Island. The parish-
ioners were headed to their seventeenth annual Sunday
picnic. It was a brilliant morning. The sun burned across
the brass instruments of the bands, across the florid
inlays of the mahogany walls. The ship rounded the
curve of Manhattan's southern tip and steamed up into
the channel, up the East River toward the Long Island
Sound. Everyone was having a good time, eating clams
and drinking beer, but as the ship neared the Harlem
River, some of the children began to complain. They
smelled smoke.

By the day's end, Captain William Van Schaick would
be in the protective custody of the New York police; he

would be blinded, with a broken leg, and have a mob howling for his blood. For now, standing in the morning sun at the bridge of the *Slocum*, he focused on a more immediate challenge. They were heading into the hardest leg of the trip, through a channel called Hell Gate.

"Hey, mister!" Twelve-year-old Frank Perditsky busted into the bridge. "The boat's on fire!"

Van Schaick shot the kid a glare, then fixed his eyes back on the river. He wasn't going in for pranks, not now, with Hell Gate churning in front of him. "You shut your trap," he told the boy. "Get out of here."

It was ten more minutes before Captain Van Schaick learned the truth. By then the fire was out of control, burning hay and fuel oil, spitting a column of black into the sky. "Full speed," he ordered, scanning for a safe berth. He had already left Manhattan behind; here the river threaded the Bronx and Queens. There were piers along both banks, but they were too dangerous, crowded with lumber and other flammable materials. He made a decision. "Put her on North Brother Island." It was just a mile ahead.

The acceleration whipped flames back along the length of the *Slocum*. The crew panicked. Old cork life preservers dissolved in the brine as the first passengers leaped over-board. For years, the owners of the *General Slocum* had ignored safety requirements and training; the lifeboats were bolted to the sides of the ship, the fire hoses were rotten. Now the burning decks swarmed with children.

North Brother came into view. It was a good choice—it had a ferry slip pier, and it housed the brand-new Riverside Hospital. They were seconds away when Van Schaick made his error.

Something caught his eye in the Bronx, and he decided

to head there instead. A moment later he thought better of it and jerked the wheel back toward the ferry slip on North Brother. The *Slocum* was going too fast for that turn; it broke the ship. Passengers were thrown across the upper deck into the guardrail, carrying it overboard.

The river boiled. Oily flames spread across its back, stewing the dead and dying. Currents battered the survivors as they swam, hauling them out to the deepest draught of the river. One boy was pulled into the water wheel. Some men returned to the breached ferry to search for children, and they had the clothes burned off their backs. Those who touched the walls fused their skin to the paint. Rescuers rushed to the scene; some fought to save lives, others robbed desperate women before helping them ashore. A few prisoners from nearby Rikers Island actually escaped so they could help in the rescue.

It remains, in this summer of 2001, the worst disaster in New York history. One thousand twenty-one persons died. As night fell, the doctors and nurses of Riverside Hospital laid out some six hundred corpses along the grassy shores of North Brother. As they worked, these doctors and nurses knew they had seen an unprecedented catastrophe. They didn't know that just three years later a new trouble would touch their shores, a trouble to eclipse the wreck of the *General Slocum*. A patient was coming to North Brother Island, a patient who would bring a hundred years of infamy.

MISSION TO NORTH BROTHER

In December 2000, Jinx classified North Brother Island a 1-9 objective: highest priority, lowest probability for success. Six months later we named it an official C-1609 goal and determined to proceed.

The difficulties of North Brother are atypical. At most targets, detection is the principal risk. North Brother offers no threat of detection, even for a daylight mission, because it is a closed site. The island is empty, abandoned for decades. It is a wildlife preserve; boats are forbidden to dock at its shores. Although well in sight of land, it faces an empty marsh in the sparse outskirts of the Bronx.

The same physical isolation that would protect us also posed the hardest challenge. How would we get there? The shortest route would be straight across the East River from the Bronx shore—a distance of perhaps two hundred yards. For weeks, Agents Brain and Illich tried to obtain a small craft we could sail across the gap. Plenty of people were happy to rent them to us—provided we stayed away from Hell Gate. The currents are too dangerous there, they told us. You don't want to sail a small boat anywhere near that channel.

We could have ignored their advice and smuggled their boats into this forbidden stretch of the river. Agent Illich is an experienced sailor, a licensed master seaman, but he himself vetoed the plan. He had run big tugboats through there enough times to know better. "Even in a strong tug, we wait for slack water before we go through Hell Gate," he said.

The solution came in a phone call from a television producer. Howard Silver, of Gotham TV, wanted to know if he could join us for an urban exploration. Sure, we told him, if you can get us to North Brother.

It took him weeks of nagging calls to the Coast Guard, the Park Service, and City Hall, but he pulled it off. We arranged to meet that Wednesday at nine A.M., at South

Street Seaport, where three Jinx agents, Silver, and his cameraman would board a patrol boat. New York's finest would chauffeur us to North Brother Island.

THE WAKE

It's a brilliant morning. Née and I stand on the pier, waiting for the others, with the whole length of Manhattan at our backs. Before us, across the East River, is the Garden Spot of the World, Brooklyn, U.S.A. The tall ships are docked around us, antique wood frigates with fresh coats of paint. Just upriver, the mighty Brooklyn Bridge rears up against the blue.

"Jinx, right?" says the man. It's Howard Silver, a small, slight man of fifty with a high pitch to his voice. He shakes our hands, introduces us to the cameraman, and tells us the boat should be along any minute.

Lefty shows up next, rocking his navy blue suit and wraparound Locs. "Lefty Leibowitz," he tells Silver, slapping him five.

Five minutes later we're down the gangplank, climbing aboard the police boat. It's a smaller boat than I expected. There's just room for us five passengers, the first mate, and our captain, Lieutenant Rodriguez of the New York Police Department's Harbor Unit. Rodriguez and his mate greet us warmly, helping us into our life vests. Sunburned and heavily tattooed, they look more like sailors than cops.

The Harbor Unit is part of the police department's Special Operations Division, home to some of the city's more interesting cops. The units that make up the division have special equipment and training. They deal with situations and environments ordinary cops can't handle. Other teams in the division include the Aviation Unit, Homeless

Outreach, Taxi Unit, and the Vandal Squad. As we leave the dock and wheel out into the East River, I have no doubt which unit I'd choose to join. The Harbor Unit acts as a last-line coast guard, providing security and rescue, making arrests, guarding the marina and the United Nations. If that weren't enough to recommend it, the Harbor Unit is also home to the scuba team, police officers who dive right here in the East River daily, searching for weapons, evidence, and bodies.

"Tell me about Jinx," says Silver, directing the cameraman to focus on Lefty. We're pulling out of the dock, headed east. We'll be following precisely the route of the *General Slocum*'s final journey.

Lefty knows the drill with the entertainment media; he drops a dose of pure propaganda. "We are the Jinx Project," he says. "We are an organization, and we are dedicated to worldwide urban adventure. We're here to explore. We're here to find out information about the urban environment, for the public good."

I lean back in my life vest and look up. We're passing beneath the Brooklyn Bridge, the first of four bridges we'll pass along our way. Riding just an arm's length off the water in this tiny craft through the yawning expanse of the river, confronting the scale of the city from sea level, distracts me from Lefty's interview. I'm almost tempted to dip my hand into the water, but this is the East River and I don't want botulism.

"Have you climbed all these bridges?" Silver asks, looking up at the Manhattan Bridge just ahead.

Lefty says, "We've climbed the Brooklyn Bridge, the Manhattan Bridge, the Williamsburg Bridge—"

"—Isn't it dangerous up there?"

"It can be," I say. "Recently I was obliged to climb the

Manhattan Bridge in the pouring rain. It's at moments like that when you examine what you're doing, and you say, 'Christ, I really am an idiot.'"

HELL GATE

Almost an hour upriver, past the Queensboro Bridge, past Roosevelt Island, I notice something strange about our captain. His eyes have narrowed slightly as he grips the wheel. His focus seems more intense.

"Everything okay?" I ask the first mate.

He smiles. "Yeah. Rodriguez just likes to play it safe up here. This is Hell Gate."

It's a bottleneck, maybe three football fields across. High above us, the Hell Gate Bridge casts its shadow.

It was 1614 when the Dutch navigator Adriaen Block first passed through this channel. He named it Hell Gate after fighting his way through to the Long Island Sound. Back then it was crowded with rocks and shoals. By the time of the *Slocum* disaster the obstacles had been cleared away, but even now Hell Gate attacks river traffic like a school of frenzied sharks. The Harlem River rushes into the East River here, where the confluence is agitated by ocean currents from the sound. Every year Hell Gate takes its tribute, running ships aground, blindsiding them with eddies that rush off Manhattan at nine knots or more.

So why is this still Hell Gate? It's been four centuries since Block wrestled the currents here. Why can't someone chart a safe route through?

I will have two questions for God: why relativity, and why turbulence. I really think he may have an answer to the first question.

Werner Heisenberg, on his deathbed

It's not for lack of attention. An almanac will give you the minute-by-minute schedule of tides, floods, and slack water for Hell Gate; your boat can hire a pilot, and if he's any good he'll know by heart every sandbar, depth, and hazard in this New York waterway. There's not a mile of the East River that isn't sounded, surveyed, and measured to provide safer navigation.

But you can't consult a book or chart for a safe route through this channel, because things simply can't be measured. The laws of fluid dynamics, elegant linear equations to predict the pressure and velocity of water, break down completely in the turbulence of Hell Gate. Here, just beneath the placid surface, runs the blender of nonlinear physics—also known as chaos. The motion of water is nondeterministic; the future location of a given molecule is not merely unknown but unknowable. It's a mystical broth—impenetrable even to the mind of God.

AMPHIBIOUS LANDING

The ferry slip that once served Riverside Hospital stands in ruins on the eastern shore of North Brother. It's high tide, but the pier is a good fifteen feet above the water. The elevator is a gutted black hulk, inoperative for decades. Rodriguez will have to drive the boat right up to the beach to drop us off. It's a matter of trial and error; the boat catches repeatedly in the soft muck as he gently traces a route to shore, cutting the engine and drifting, then starting up again in reverse. Finally he brings the boat in as close as he can—just four or five feet from the beach. I climb to the front of the boat and jump to the sand. Lefty jumps next, then the cameraman, and then Silver, who lands wrong and hurts his foot.

Renée sees Silver's painful limp and decides not to jump ashore. She slips off her shoes, hangs off the slide, and drops into the gentle surf. I shudder to watch her splash through that East River water in her bare feet.

We climb up onto the pier from the beach and watch Rodriguez pull away. He's leaving us free rein over the island; he'll return at four in the afternoon to pick us up. The pier looks worse from above than from below; half a century's disrepair has rotted it through. Turning away from the river, we can now see the remains of the original Riverside Hospital. There are three brick buildings, half-obscured by the thick tree covering, connected by dirt roads.

The closest building, we will learn, is the old hospital, where the survivors of the *Slocum* were treated. It looks sound enough, especially compared to the second building, which has trees growing through its roof. This is the boiler house, overlooked by a hundred-foot brick smokestack. The third building is much smaller, probably used for storage.

We head up to the boiler house first, intrigued by its horrendous state of repair. A strong kick opens the door. "Jesus Christ," says Lefty, stepping inside. The whole interior is a single room, floored with gray dust and broken glass. Light streams through the trees and what's left of the roof. A furnace almost fills the entire two-story space. Its ovens lie cold and open, ash cascading out of them to the floor. Catwalks line the ceiling, some of them unhinged and hanging loose. The place looks like a crematorium.

We move cautiously to the back. There's a flooded stairwell leading to a cellar; leaves float in its mirrored surface. Through the back, we enter the thick under-brush of the forest. The smokestack is here, towering ten stories above the trees. A ladder runs up its side, but it's blocked by a knot of thick vines—I won't get to climb this chimney.

"Look over here," says Howard Silver. He's found a collecting pool, perhaps fifty feet across, hidden there in the woods. It's a stone well with sides three feet high.

"Don't step on the nest," Renée tells Lefty. She's pointing to an egret nest, almost invisible there in the under-growth, the first of many we'll see today. The eggs are large and speckled. Lefty backs away slowly. This is a pro-tected nesting ground for egrets, and we've given assur-ances to the Harbor Unit that we'll avoid them with care.

"Let's get out of all this goddamned nature," I tell the group. "I want to check out the hospital."

The hospital door opens out. It's not locked, but there's so much debris at its base I have to jerk hard at it to get inside. The building looks like an apartment house. It's surprisingly small: two stories, room perhaps for two hundred patients. There's something distinctly feminine in the atmosphere; as we move toward the back we see a dressing screen and then an antique gynecological table.

"They examined her here," Renée says, shining her flashlight on the iron table's stirrups.

No one has yet spoken the name, but Renée's talking about the witch of North Brother Island.

TYPHOID MARY

Typhoid has always been a disease of poverty. It lives through filthy slums, percolating in backed-up sewers. So when it breached the summer home of Charles

Henry Warren, infecting five from his family and staff, the disease achieved a new eminence: It was now a high-class affliction. A sanitation engineer, Dr. George Soper, determined to find the source of this new contamination. He began finding reports of similar incidents: well-to-do households suddenly stricken, with no explanation found. There was a common link through all these households. A huge woman of forty, broad-shouldered and statuesque, had supervised each household's kitchen as cook. She had disappeared after every outbreak and had gone by many names. After months of investigation Soper learned her identity and where she was employed. In March 1907 he made a visit to a Park Avenue residence, too late for the daughter of the house, who was about to succumb to typhoid fever. There he first laid eyes on Mary Mallon.

> I had my first talk with Mary in the kitchen of the house. I suppose it was an unusual kind of interview, particularly when the place is taken into consideration. I was as diplomatic as possible, but I had to say I suspected her of making people sick, and that I wanted specimens of her urine, feces, and blood.
>
> She seized a carving fork and advanced in my direction. I passed rapidly down the long, narrow hall, through the tall iron gate, out through the area, and so to the sidewalk. I felt rather lucky to escape.

(From *The Peculiar Case of Typhoid Mary*, by Dr. George Soper)

Soper made another attempt to bring her in, visiting her at her home, before admitting she was more than he could handle. He was an academic, bookish and cerebral. She was a Irish immigrant from the slums who had escaped starvation in her home country and survived by her wits in New York. She was stronger than Soper, tougher, and an expert with cutlery. He called the police.

Her arrest, a few days later, justified the doctor's apprehension. Mary did not intend to go quietly. She slammed the door in the first cop's face when they came for her at the house where she worked. She jetted through a back entrance, hopped a tall fence, and barricaded herself in a neighbor's outhouse. When they found her and forced open the door, they faced a cornered fugitive. It took five cops to restrain and capture her; she kept spitting, cursing, and fighting all the way to Riverside Hospital.

I am an innocent human being.

"Typhoid" Mary Mallon, 1907

A four-century period of European history, ending in the eighteenth century but reaching its peak at around 1600 A.D., is called the Burning Times. It was during this period that civil and religious authorities, mostly in Germany, France, and Switzerland, committed a holocaust. They hanged or burned alive almost one hundred thousand suspected witches, three out of four of whom were women.

The accused were called whores of Satan. Animal servants called familiars were said to assist the witches in their black rites. A trial for witchcraft included a thorough physical examination of the defendant. They were searching for the devil's mark, a mole, a scar, or some other blemish on the skin. It was through this mark, the judges claimed, a witch nursed her familiar with mother's milk. No other aspect of witch trials was more degrading to a defendant than this examination. The hidden areas of a woman's body received special scrutiny: the breasts, thighs, buttocks, and especially the sexual organs would be studied for devil's marks.

The examiners' medieval knowledge of anatomy led to thousands of false positives. Joseph Klaits writes in *Servants of Satan: The Age of the Witch Hunts*:

> One witch suspect in the Swiss canton of Fribourg contemptuously chided her judges for their naïveté about female anatomy. After the prosecutors discovered what they took to be a devil's mark on her genitals, Erni Vufflod informed them that "if this was a sign of witchcraft, many women would be witches."

Mary Mallon shared that suspect's contempt for her captors. The doctors described her as intelligent but capable of "almost pathological anger." She ridiculed their unseemly fascination with her feces. In the first year she stayed in Riverside, they collected samples three times a week. Most of the time, the results demonstrated her body simmering with typhoid, but for weeks at a time they came back negative. They suggested taking out her gall bladder, but admitted it might not do any good. "No . . ." she told them, "no knife will be put on me." Mary was not, in fact, ill. She was a carrier of the germ, but not a sufferer. She soon realized these doctors were as naïve as the Fribourg judges in their efforts to "cure" her. "In spite of the medical staff," wrote Mary in an affidavit,

> Dr. Wilson ordered me Urotropin . . . I got that on and off for a year . . . if I had continued it would certainly have killed me for it was very Severe. Every one knows who is acquainted in

any kind of medicine that it's used for *Kidney* trouble? I have been in fact a peep show.

In the room adjacent to the examination theater I find a laboratory. It's small, with a sink and some cabinets. "Check this out," I tell Renée and Lefty, shining my flashlight over the faded jar labels. I open a jar, and spill some sort of black soot over my sleeve. How many tests did they run in this little room, sampling and recording Mary Mallon's bacteria count? What were they trying to find out? They knew she carried typhoid and they knew they couldn't cure her. Why did they persist in collecting evidence? On June 20, 1909, the *New York American* ran a cartoon of Mary at her stove, dropping human skulls into a skillet. Mary took to carrying the cartoon around with her in her pocket.

THE GROUNDS

We head back out into the sunshine. The sky swarms with birds, more birds than you'd see in a year.

We head through the storehouse into the woods behind it. An incongruous fire plug stands there in the undergrowth. Green is everywhere. Ahead we see a house, standing alone in this heavy forest, without a road or path leading to it. The house is one story tall, but it has a high gabled roof and an impressive cedar porch. We swing around to the side. The porch hangs decimated; splintered boards, bolts, nails, and glass pile over its sides to the ground at our feet. We gingerly climb up, balancing on the sturdier planks.

A huge book rests in the midst of all this devastation, on its own pedestal in the middle of the porch. Renée opens it and blows away the dust. It's a ledger, filled out in the gorgeous script that was once requisite to the bookkeeping profession. "It's the daily records," Renée says. "'Baked beans, tomato soup, clam chowder, vanilla extract.'"

Lefty heads into the house. It's a gutted, empty room with spray paint on the walls. In the dust and garbage of the floor, another egret has built her nest; it sleeps seven eggs. Stepping to the window, Lefty sees the new hospital.

"Hey," he says, rushing back to the porch. "There's another building. It's big."

The rehabilitation center, a 152-bed facility, opened in 1952 to treat teenage drug addicts. It was the first-ever major project to combine medical treatment with psychological care and education. The city predicted it would eliminate teenage drug use within five years. It stands there before us as the remains of North Brother's final disaster.

This was supposed to be a medical center, with patients referred by area hospitals. Instead, it became a de facto prison, populated by hardcore ghetto junkies sent here by the courts. The evils of the prison system festered here—gangs self-segregating along race lines, contraband smuggled and sold, with guards taking their cut. An addict coming here with hope of recovery would soon despair, trapped on an unkempt, overgrown island awash in drugs and prostitution. Several patients drowned trying to escape.

The evidence is all around us as we search through the seven-story brick building. Whole rooms are caged off with steel grates. Graffiti desecrates the walls: "The nurses let you fuck them in the ass." More bizarre are the paintings, surrealist fresco works incorporating a row of holes in the walls, so that you can look through and see one painting within another. The themes are weeping eyes and birds, cartoon sunsets, and blood.

PUBLIC HEALTH

There's a coloring book on the floor of the fifth-story corridor. I pick it up. "It's written at a child's level," I tell the others, and read from it. "'John went out with Mary. He caught Syphilis from her! Syphilis is spread by sexual intercourse.'" The illustrations are charming; you'd never suspect these guys and dolls, dressed in prewar styles, were unclean syphilitics.

The syphilis coloring book epitomizes the broad array of sciences, services, and disciplines collectively called public health. Epidemiology, the statistical science that charts the spread of disease through populations, is a core feature of public health, along with preventative medicine, occupational safety, disease control, sanitary engineering, and health education. Public health recommendations are often legislated—the sign that tells you not to spit on the subway is left over from the war on tuberculosis.

Between the lines of this syphilis Dick-and-Jane is a sophisticated attack on a central public health problem—infectious diseases are, and always have been, endemic among the uneducated lower classes. Dr. Soper's *Peculiar Case* describes an outbreak of typhoid among the rural poor:

> . . . one person in ten was sick, and one person in a hundred was dying of the disease. You have no idea of the state of mind I found the people in. They didn't know what to do; didn't know where to go; didn't know whom to suspect and whom to trust . . .

Public health agencies like the Centers for Disease Control seek to saturate even the darkest corners of poverty with information. They publish pamphlets and brochures, in dozens of languages, describing the diseases that threaten communities; they list symptoms, hazards, means of infection, and how to seek treatment. Public health is an unglamorous field: Many of its frontline soldiers are neither doctors nor scientists, and their efforts rarely make the headlines. It's too bad because public health has saved more lives, by a factor of a hundred, than all the doctors and drugs in the world. Education and sanitation alone can short-circuit an epidemic.

TYPHOID

Typhoid is information. It is a message, encoded in the genes of the bacterium *Salmonella typhi*. Its message is essentially the same as any genetic code's: Copy me. The bacteria only infect humans. They flourish in the bloodstream, colonize the intestinal tract and the gallbladder. The symptoms are sustained high fever, weakness, pain, rash, and complications that lead to death in one of five cases.

Typhoid communicates its code only one way—through feces. In countries like Mexico, where the water is contaminated with sewage, typhoid is endemic and growing stronger. Over twelve million persons are stricken with typhoid every year in the developing world. When an infected person goes to the bathroom and fails to wash his hands, he creates an invisible culture of typhoid on his fingers and under his nails. If that person shakes your hand or prepares your food, you will receive the message.

Medicine alone cannot stop typhoid. The abuse of

antibiotics, overprescription, and the failure of patients to complete their course of treatment has created drug-resistant strains—the majority of North American typhoid strains are now immune to antibiotics. The eradication of typhoid can only come through sanitation, epidemic tracking, quarantine, and education.

A disease lives through a population, flaring up in small groups here and there, building strength and momentum where conditions favor it. It moves in currents, frequencies that can be measured in wavelength and modulation. As the frequencies build in strength, they interfere with each other, transferring large energy movements into small ones. This is turbulence; the same mathematics governing the churn of Hell Gate describe the spread of typhoid. In this witch's brew of chaos, nature hides the trail of causation. To this day no one knows how many people Typhoid Mary infected or how many she killed.

ESCAPE FROM NORTH BROTHER ISLAND

"What makes a place worth exploring?" Silver asks. We're on the roof of the rehabilitation center, high above the trees. From here we can see the whole island, abandoned, overgrown. The birds swarm through the air around us, screaming in the afternoon light.

"It has to be off-limits," I tell the camera, "merely because if it were not off-limits, then everyone would be there, and if everyone were there, then it wouldn't be virgin territory for our explorations."

Lefty says, "We want to explore someplace that is beyond the vision or beyond ordinary experience."

Renée has unpacked the flag; she hands it to me.

There's no place to hang it, so I stand up on the ledge and hold it up in the strong wind. It doesn't feel like much of a conquest. Our garrison looks down on nothing but ruin and the ghosts of suffering bastards.

"How do you feel about the police?" asks Silver.

I jump down from the ledge and start to pack up the flag. "We like the police. We don't have any problem with them. They do a great service, at great risk, and with little thanks. Even when they arrested us years ago, we felt no resentment. We break the law when we explore, so we know they have to try to stop us. But we're not practicing civil disobedience.

"These are not unjust laws. These laws are for the public safety, for the protection of the general population. We just don't feel that they apply to us." I hand the flag back to Renée. "We're highly trained professionals."

We head back to the pier and begin waiting for our ride home. It's blazing hot, and the insects plague my sunburned neck. Half an hour passes; everyone's too tired for conversation. We sit and watch the still water.

Typhoid Mary left Riverside Hospital in 1910. The health commissioner had ordered her release. "She has been released," he said, "because she has been shut up long enough to learn the precautions she ought to take." Chief among those precautions was that she must never work as a cook. The state found her a job as a laundress; this was an unskilled position, with a much lower salary than she had earned as a cook. She quit the job and disappeared.

Five years later, Dr. Soper took a call from the head obstetrician and gynecologist at Manhattan's Sloane Hospital for Women.

[He] telephoned me asking that I come at once to the hospital to see him about a matter of great importance. When I arrived there, he said that he had a typhoid epidemic of more than twenty cases on his hands. The other servants had jokingly nicknamed a cook "Typhoid Mary." She was out at the moment, but would I recognize her handwriting if she really was that woman? He handed me a letter, from which I saw at once that the cook was indeed Mary Mallon, and I also identified her from his description. I advised that the Health Department be notified, and it was not long before Mary was again taken and sent to North Brother Island.

Mary had spent the past five years scuttling across New York, cooking under assumed names, spreading her contagion. Now she was back on North Brother for good. She had rekindled the old instincts of the Burning Times, the panicked fascination with feminine mystery. But there was a difference. The victims of the witch trials had been falsely accused; they were innocents and had done no harm. Typhoid Mary had knowingly spread misery and death from her kitchen. She died on North Brother twenty-three years later.

When the patrol boat arrives, we discover the tide is out. Rodriguez can't bring the boat in to the shore; he's hitting the bottom about twenty yards out. He'll wait a half hour to let the water rise. By now I'm beginning to think I'll die of old age on North Brother as Mary did.

The wait, as it happens, is in vain. The depth doesn't change significantly.

"What are we going to do?" I ask Lefty.

"We're going to have to wade out to the boat." Lefty already has his shoes off and is rolling up his pants.

I cringed this morning to see Renée take two steps through this water. Now I begin to wade out into it.

I hold my suit pants, shoes, and socks above the surface. The riverbed is a soft, frigid muck that sucks down at my feet. We trudge slowly through the currents, perhaps fifty paces from shore. By the time we get to the boat we're waist-deep in the East River.

THE NEW YORK AIRSPACE, in the summer of 2001, contains twenty-five of the world's hundred tallest buildings. The Empire State Building, the world's most famous skyscraper, towers 1,250 feet over the city and occupies 37 million square feet of sky. It is overlooked by the World Trade Center, whose first tower tops off at 1,368 feet. Both One World Trade Center and the Empire State Building sport powerful antennae.

New York's skies crackle with broadcast signals from six local television stations, fifty-three local radio stations, tens of millions of cell phones, walkie-talkies, citizen's band, crystal, and short-wave radios.

Over this crowd of rooftops and antennae fly hundreds of commercial jets and dozens of helicopters each day. Joining them are small aircraft, military planes, and occasionally the Goodyear blimp. Most of this traffic is headed to or from New York City's two major airports, LaGuardia and John F. Kennedy International. JFK, the larger of the two at 344 acres, is the world's busiest cargo airport.

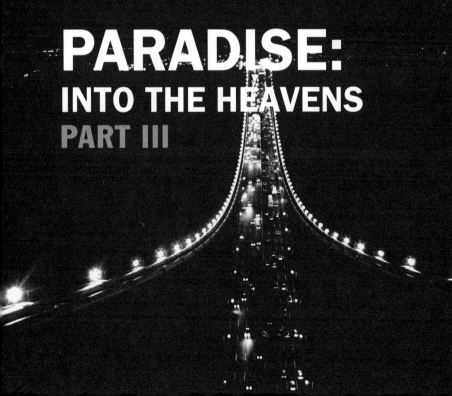

PARADISE:
INTO THE HEAVENS
PART III

ELEVEN THE BRIDGE OF
BLACKWELL'S ISLAND:
THE QUEENSBORO BRIDGE

<table>
<tr><td style="vertical-align: top; writing-mode: vertical-rl;">Attach label, or print or type</td><td>

Mission
THE QUEENSBORO BRIDGE

Location
EAST RIVER, BETWEEN MANHATTAN'S SECOND AVENUE AND
FIFTY-NINTH STREET AND QUEENS' LONG ISLAND CITY

Goal
TO CLIMB THE LAST OF THE CITY'S EAST RIVER BRIDGES
AND TO DISPLAY THE JINX FLAG AT ITS HIGHEST POINT

Officers
LEFTY LEIBOWITZ, L. B. DEYO

Team
BRAIN, JOSH, SPECIAL AGENT RENÉE, MIKE, PABLO, FRANK

</td></tr>
</table>

REPORTED BY ▼

Lefty Leibowitz

Lefty

With great power comes great responsibility.

Spider-Man

BRAIN AND I WALK EAST on the pedestrian walkway of Manhattan's Queensboro Bridge, stopping every few moments to look for a way to access the maintenance ladders that tower more than one hundred feet above our heads. Brain is clutching a single sheet of paper in his hands. It's a map that our associate Agent Bleach drew while visiting the bridge on an earlier reconnaissance mission. In crude handwriting, the map shows the location of the bridge's main towers in relation to its entranceway, roadways, and pinnacle. It does not show *how* to get to the bridge's highest point, though—we will have to find that out on our own during the course of today's mission. So far we have not had any luck. The rest of the team—L.B., Renée, Josh, and Mike—are about two hundred yards closer to Manhattan, having paused near a high scaffolding alongside the westernmost tower that is the most likely candidate for climbing. They are accompanied by Pablo and Frank, a cameraman and reporter from the Travel Channel who are here to gather footage for an upcoming feature on urban exploration.

We are assembled this warm July evening for the purpose of climbing this bridge, the only one of the four great East River bridges that we have yet to climb. The Williamsburg, Manhattan, and Brooklyn Bridges have in the past all been sites of Jinx explorations. It was a story about our climb of the Broadway Bridge spanning the Harlem River that first began to build the Jinx Project's reputation as the premier exponent of urban exploration in the world. Of the major commuter bridges that served the city, only the Queensboro, Triboro, and George Washington Bridges remain to be climbed.

A SHORT HISTORY OF THE BRIDGE

The Queensboro, or 59th Street, Bridge was the last of several attempts to build a bridge between Manhattan and southern Queens. As early as 1838, proposals were made for a multi-span suspension bridge that would go over Blackwell's Island (now Roosevelt Island) to Long Island City. Almost twenty years later, John Roebling proposed his own plan, but again progress was stalled. Roebling continued to press for the Blackwell's Island Bridge, but also proposed a bridge between Brooklyn and lower Manhattan. In 1867 the charters for the creation of the Brooklyn Bridge and Blackwell's Island Bridge were given. The plans for the Brooklyn Bridge moved forward, but concerns about the low population density in Queens caused the company in charge of the Blackwell's Island Bridge to go bankrupt in 1893.

Finally, in 1902, a bridge engineer by the name of Gustav Lindenthal was put in charge of the project by the mayor. He proposed a twin cantilever design and a total length of 7,449 feet. Four steel towers, each 350 feet tall and placed on stone piers, would provide support.

The project began in earnest, but there were still problems. When Mayor George B. McClellan, a Tammany loyalist, took over, he replaced Lindenthal with one of his own men. An uncompleted section of the bridge collapsed in a windstorm. Union saboteurs dynamited the span, angered by the project's open-shop policy. A lengthy steel strike, and yet another cantilever collapse, didn't help.

The bridge didn't open to the public until March 30, 1909. It had cost twenty million dollars and fifty lives. Despite all the difficulties, its opening was celebrated with a huge fireworks extravaganza, and the bridge took its place in those early years as the pinnacle of good taste and class. In *The Great Gatsby,* socialites and millionaires use the bridge to travel between their Manhattan and Long Island homes. Though the bridge does not have the same élan today, it is still a key point of departure for city dwellers on their way to the Queens and Long Island suburbs.

THE ASCENT BEGINS

But the question remains: How will we find a way to climb it? On some bridges in the city, there are easily accessible maintenance ladders and stairways that can carry explorers to the bridge's apex with minimal athleticism required. The only real obstacles to success are an explorer's innate fear of heights and the potential for entanglement with the authorities. The climb itself is as simple as walking up a flight of stairs.

In other cases it's not so easy. The Brooklyn Bridge, for example, has no ladder or stairway for maintenance workers, only a suspension cable that spans the length of the bridge and arches slowly to its highest point. The only way to get to the top is to walk up that suspension cable one step at a time.

Brain and I return to the group with bad news. We have walked the entire length of the pedestrian walkway, but we haven't found an entryway. Even the "neat and detailed" drawn map that Agent Bleach has supplied us with has not helped.

"There's nothing," Brain says dejectedly. We thought we had found a portal to an internal ladder in one of the beams, but when we tried to open it, it was welded shut. The only way to get in is with a blowtorch.

"He's right," I follow. "The only way to get to the top of this bridge will be to climb up this scaffolding."

Josh swallows hard as he stares at the rickety structure that lies before him. It seems to be swaying in the wind and is bound to the structure of the bridge at only one point, about one hundred feet up.

"We're going to have to give it a try," L.B. tells the others. "Who's coming and who wants to stay on ground patrol?"

I raise my hand to nominate myself for the climb. Josh and Mike's hands follow a split second later. Brain and Renée decide to keep a lookout at the base of the scaffolding. Pablo and Frank smile wide, their teeth flashing in the neon's glow. They are forbidden by their employers to do anything that might endanger the expensive camera equipment they've brought along tonight, they tell us. They don't look overly disappointed for this blessed excuse to keep their feet planted on the ground.

I begin to examine the scaffolding, looking for a place to begin the ascent. Inside the beams that support the higher levels of the bridge is a latticework of iron forming perpendicular crisscrosses of metal that resemble a ladder. I motion to the others.

"I think we'd be better off climbing up there and then moving onto the scaffolding on the next level," I tell them.

The others nod in agreement, and before anyone can reply, L.B. leaps onto the iron beam and begins working his way upward. We watch as L.B. searches for grips and footholds amidst the metalwork.

L.B. makes some progress on his climb, and then I jump onto the beam and begin my own ascent, followed by Josh and Mike. It's a short climb to the base of the scaffolding, and in a series of movements each of us ducks through the metal pipes and finds himself standing on a wooden platform at the base of the scaffolding's long and winding staircase.

Now up on the scaffolding, I feel exactly how flimsy the structure is. The entire edifice is constructed of thin, round metal poles, like the ones that provide support at either end of a garden-variety chain-link fence. A stairwell is built into the center of the scaffolding and climbs up toward the apex of the bridge in seven sections.

"Do you think this thing can hold all of our weight?" I ask the others. I have my doubts. Every time someone takes a step or shifts his weight, I can feel the entire network of pipes and stairs tremble. I want to get to the top fast. I'll feel a lot more secure when we get back onto the main structure of the bridge.

Step by step we ascend the stairwell. Soon we are above the pedestrian walkway and even with the lower level of car traffic on the bridge. We are enveloped in the long shadows that the bridge creates at this late hour, and I feel secure that none of the motorists hurtling by can see us in the darkness.

THE QUESTION OF THE MEDIA

Back on the pedestrian walkway, I find out later, Pablo and Frank are interviewing Renée and Brain. The presence of the media in the urban exploration world is controversial, and with some justification. Too many explorers are willing to exchange sensitive information for a glimpse of fame, even to the point of revealing hidden locations that are better left unshared with the public at large.

This is a tightrope that we have tried to walk carefully at Jinx. On one hand, it is our duty as explorers to announce our discoveries. Otherwise, what good can come of them? Did Columbus keep quiet about America? Did Armstrong keep quiet about the moon?

On the other hand, we don't want to jeopardize secret locations that are held in high esteem by others in our field. For that reason, we focus on well-known places and landmarks in New York City. Not many people will be surprised to hear of the existence of the top of the Queensboro Bridge, but we have an opportunity to show them a different side of it via our explorations.

Another issue that comes up in dealing with the press is the tendency to sensationalize urban exploration and its allure. Stories that glorify the aspect of machismo and recklessness do little to help the efforts of responsible explorers who speak of its intellectual appeal but are still cognizant of its dangers.

Pablo and Frank seem like good guys, but I am wary of their attempts to have us pose for pictures and create narratives for their story. Over the course of the evening they would attempt to stage shots and put words in our mouths. We remain polite, but firmly stand our ground and refuse to be anything but ourselves.

We've decided it's better to talk with the press and to guide them to a correct understanding of UE. By answering the media's questions, we can accurately explain why we explore. The alternative is to allow an ignorant and sensationalistic press to churn out copy of their own accord, without the mediating influence of people who are protective of the topic at hand.

ONLY THE DIEHARDS REMAIN

A few more flights and the four of us are now even with the upper level of traffic. A few more, and we reach the end of the staircase. We are standing on a catwalk that spans the width of the bridge from north to south. To our left and also to our right, the bridge slopes upward to the two adjacent towers. For the first one hundred yards or so it is a gentle slope, no steeper than the inclines on many New York City sidewalks. At the one-hundred-yard mark, however, the slope swerves violently upward to a near thirty-degree angle before reaching the towers.

There is no walkway from the catwalk to the tower— only a thick, flat cable flanked by two thin suspension wires. The climb is about to get much harder.

We pause for a few moments to catch our breath. Josh and Mike take photos while L.B. and I examine the beam that leads up to the tower.

"Who's coming with me to the tower?" L.B. asks us.

"This is as far as I go," Mike replies. "I'll take a bunch of photos from here, but you're not gonna catch me walking on that cable. You can tell me about it when you get back."

"*If* he gets back," Josh mutters to himself.

"I'll stay on the catwalk," I say. From this point, I'll be able to keep an eye on L.B. as he heads toward the apex and also watch the goings-on with the rest of the explorers on the ground. As far as I'm concerned, the proposition of climbing on the cables to the next tower is insane and stupid. It's also scary as hell. I've been to the tops of bridges before, but I've never been able to escape the sense of dread that forms in the pit of my stomach when I look down over the city from four hundred feet. And the challenge before us today is particularly horrifying—it's just us and the bridge, no ladders or stairways here. We've never used climbing equipment on our expeditions, but today I sure wish we had some grappling hooks and safety cables for L.B. to use.

"So be it," L.B. says. I've just become convinced of something I've suspected for a long time: He's got a death wish, especially on missions involving heights. He begins strapping an extra camera around his neck so he can take photos once he reaches the tower, providing he is able to do so before falling to his demise. He also begins folding up the Jinx flag and tucks it into my messenger bag, which he has borrowed from me for his ascent. With a final glance back toward Josh, Mike, and me and then one more toward Brain and Renée two hundred yards below, L.B. hops over the small metal gate that separates the north-south catwalk from the sloping cable that leads up to the tower.

Josh and Mike snap a few more pictures and then begin to descend the rickety scaffolding to rejoin the others on the pedestrian walkway. I wait where I am and watch.

AT THE PINNACLE

L.B. is by himself now, balancing on the metal beam that ascends to the bridge's pinnacle. He is about twenty feet from the metal catwalk where he left behind the rest of us. The beam he's standing on is about eight inches wide. To his left and right are thin metal guide wires that follow the beam to the top. Aside from that, there is the warm, sticky air of August on all sides and a long drop to the East River.

Back on the pedestrian walkway, Josh, Mike, Renée, Brain, Pablo, and Frank stand with their necks craned toward the sky. They're unable to see either L.B. or me. The explorers on the ground wait, not knowing what is happening, or who is alive or dead. Pablo and Frank are running their cameras.

Laughing Boy continues forward, carefully placing one foot in front of the other. He keeps a close grip on the guide wires that are on either side of him. So far, so good, but he is approaching the portion of the climb where the cable starts to dramatically increase its angle of incline. He crawls over a crossbeam that is blocking his path and regains his footing on the cable.

As I watch his climb, perched from my location above the highway traffic, I see a small black object fall from L.B.'s vicinity into the roadway below, where it is annihilated by an oncoming truck. I later find out that it was his sunglasses—they had slipped from his face as he looked down to guide his feet along the cable.

As he pushes ahead, I think about the bridges we've climbed in the past and the feelings we've attained upon concluding a successful climb. Even sitting on this catwalk, far from the pinnacle but much farther from the walkway below, I am halfway between nausea and elation. I hope that L.B. won't take any unnecessary risks on his way to the top. As if any of this is necessary in the first place. I grip the cool metal of the catwalk tight and try to slow my breathing.

Laughing Boy pulls himself up the ever-increasing incline. He's getting close to the top now, close enough that success seems like a real possibility. Just a few more feet and he'll be able to pull himself up onto the tower's walkway and hang the Jinx flag.

Meanwhile, I continue to stand on the catwalk watching Laughing Boy's progress. I am prepared to shout down to the others in case of an emergency, but so far it looks as if L.B.'s going to make it. I want Pablo and Frank's story to be exciting, but I hope that the excitement does not extend to L.B.'s disfigurement.

Laughing Boy is standing on the tower's walkway now, having safely navigated the arcing beam all the way to its pinnacle. He fumbles with the messenger bag and clumsily pulls out the Jinx flag folded neatly in its front pocket. It is now time for the coup de grâce. He holds up the flag proudly and admires the sprawling cityscape laid out like a canvas before his eyes. The adrenaline of the moment hides the fatigue of his body as he searches the darkness below with his eyes. He can make out Renée, Brain, and the others on the walkway below, but they don't see him.

"Damn," I think to myself. The flag picture is the culmination of a Jinx mission. It is the only souvenir that we will have from our adventure today, and a key element in our empirical data set.

L.B. waves the flag some more and waits where the team below can most easily see him. Still nothing. He continues waiting. One minute passes, then another, then another. There is nothing he can do to grab their attention except to continue to stand there. We'll have to wait here until somebody decides to look up. God knows how long that could take.

On the walkway below, Renée stands with Mike and Josh, eyes turned toward the sky. Pablo and Frank are smoking cigarettes, bored. Brain has wandered off down the bridge to find a better view of the activity on the tower. No one has seen or heard anything from L.B. or myself in approximately twenty minutes. Anxiety fills the air, though no one will admit it to themselves or the others.

As Brain reaches the base of the adjacent tower, he looks upward and scans the darkness for any sign of motion. Nothing. He is not able to see either L.B. or myself nestled in the darkness. He is worried now for his fellow explorers and their safe return.

Suddenly, he sees a flash of yellow high above him. "Guys! Get over here! I see him!" he yells to the others.

Renée, Josh, and Mike come running toward Brain. Pablo and Frank are several steps behind as they simultaneously try to break into a run and start their cameras.

In the glow of New York's nighttime lights, the explorers see the flag of Jinx waving slowly in the distance. The yellow triangle and exclamation point can clearly be made out against the black backdrop. Soon the cameras come out, and the whirrs and clicks of the shutters ensure the successful climax of our journey.

TWELVE

THE CENTER OF THE UNIVERSE: ⚠️
THE GEORGE WASHINGTON BRIDGE

Attach label, or print or type

Mission
GEORGE WASHINGTON BRIDGE, LATE SUMMER 2001

Location
FORT WASHINGTON, HUDSON RIVER SHORE

Goal
SUMMIT

Officers
LEFTY LEIBOWITZ, L. B. DEYO

Team
STEVE DUNCAN, AGENT ILLICH, JOSH, SPECIAL AGENT
RENÉE, MIKE

REPORTED BY ▼

L. B. Deyo

L. B. Deyo

. . . New York City. Or as I like to call it, the Center of the Universe.

Mayor Rudolph Guiliani

THE GRID

It is impossible not to feel stirred at the thought of men at certain historic moments of adventure and discovery—Columbus when he first saw the Western shore, Pizarro when he stared at the Pacific Ocean, Franklin when the electric spark came from the string of his kite, Galileo when he first turned his telescope to the heavens. Such moments are granted to students in the abstract regions of thought, and high among them must be placed the morning when Descartes lay in his bed and invented the method of coordinate geometry.

Alfred North Whitehead

The attentive reader will notice that this is the last chapter of the book. Having set out in search of New York, how close are we to finding it? Finding something means, at the very least, being able to say where it is. How can we locate the city, and how can we describe its position?

René Descartes, a twenty-four-year-old officer in the Dutch army, was kept awake at night by such questions. The proofs and methods of classical geometry, so beautifully consistent and thorough, remained incompatible with post-classical mathematics; it handled shapes in the abstract, without reference to their positions. There was no way to combine algebra with geometry, and there was no efficient means to translate geometric knowledge to real-world problems. Artillery spotters needed to plot the curves of shells through the air, for example, but how to translate the motion of real objects through space into the language of numbers? To calculate a projectile's arc, one needed to input the location of the cannon, know the location of the target, and then plot the points through which the cannonball would pass. All of this was impossible. No one had invented a way to mathematically describe the location of an object in space.

One day in 1619, Descartes lay half-awake, staring at a spider's web, when he hit on the solution. He would impose a grid on the Euclidean plane; a map of numbered lines extending out from a single origin. Each point on the plane could then be located by its position on the X and Y axes and be described by just two numbers, its coordinates. All the shapes and lines of geometry could be transcribed to algebra, and measurements in the real world could be calculated. This elegant solution was the basis for modern mathematics; it was the most important discovery since those of ancient Greece.

Sir Isaac Newton took Descartes's mathematics and applied them to the universe. He laid the grid across the stars and planets, assigning coordinates to the heavenly bodies, transforming their movements into lines and curves, algebraic functions and physical laws. This digitization of space was based on an assumption: that the universe is as orderly as a sheet of graph paper. It was the vision of a cosmic grid, eternal and absolute. In Newton's physics, up is up, down is down, and any spot in the universe has its own fixed coordinates.

Einstein, slacking off at his post in the patent office,

brought down this eternal grid. His Special Theory of Relativity proved that nothing in the universe had an absolute position. A place could be near or far, up or down, left or right, only in relation to something else. Instead of each having permanent coordinates, any point could now be an origin, 0,0.

The consequences of Einstein's discovery were disturbing. Everyone now began thinking in relative terms. People misapplied the physical relativity of space to the world of morality—the result was the twentieth century. Whatever special significance we might still have held for the planet Earth, we could no longer say it held a special place in the universe. Worst of all, there could remain no physical basis for Mayor Rudolph Guiliani's claim that New York City was the center of the universe.

LOCAL GROUP, JULY 16, 1609

So, we can't say we know where New York is in absolute terms. If we're going to find it, we have to find it using local landmarks and place it in relation to them. From the general to the particular, we can first say that New York is to be found in the Local Group.

The Local Group is a cluster of twenty galaxies. Its borders are fuzzy; its perimeter is only a shifting haze of stars at the outer edges of its outermost galaxies. Along an arbitrary axis, it's roughly 10 million light years across.

At first glance, this is an odd place for a city. The Local Group is mostly empty space (more than 99.999 percent empty), very cold and awash in deadly microwave radiation left over from the Big Bang. But New York is here, in the flickering light of the first galaxy on the left.

THE MILKY WAY, JULY 16, 1609

This galaxy is typical; a whirlpool of a hundred billion stars with an invisible supermassive black hole at the center. Looking at the Milky Way, we might worry whether we can find a city amid all these stars. Luckily, the choice is far narrower than it appears. In addition to the background radiation of the Local Group, a second surge of lethal rays radiates from the swollen thermonuclear blur at the whirlpool's center. This radiation is so fierce that nothing could survive on most of the stars in the galaxy; life could only have emerged in the distant hinterlands farthest from the center.

Sure enough, New York is here, on the outer spiral arm. The radiation here is far weaker. Still, it's too much for terrestrial life to cope with. If an astronaut could reach interstellar space, her ship must have thick lead shields to keep her from being cooked alive. Fortunately, New York has its own radiation shield: the solar system.

THE SOLAR SYSTEM, JULY 16, 1609

For a long time, scientists thought the solar system was just the sun, the planets, some moons, and the odd asteroid or comet. Until recently, the orbit of Pluto was thought to be at the outer edge of the solar system. Now, though, most astronomers agree the solar system goes on for trillions of miles beyond the planets, extending to a sphere around the sun almost a light year into space. At the edge of this sphere is a hypothetical layer of comets called the Oort Cloud. Here the comets, billions in number, are believed to orbit endlessly around the sun, so far out we can't yet directly detect them. What keeps them out here, like the lining of a balloon? Why don't they fall in toward the sun, or drift out into interstellar space?

They are attracted to the sun, like all objects in the solar system, by its gravity. Oort Cloud comets are also repulsed by the sun. The sun's magnetic field holds them out here in permanent exile. This same magnetic field also protects the moons and planets from the punishing rays of interstellar space; it acts like an ozone layer to the whole solar system.

Of course, we do see comets nearby from time to time. A rare cosmic ray will penetrate the magnetic field and strike a comet hard enough to send it careering toward the sun. In the early eons of the system, the sky teemed with such stray objects. The moon, having no erosion from wind or rain, still bears the scars of past bombardment. Even now, though, stray comets and asteroids are a great hazard to life. How is it New York has evolved in this shooting gallery?

One answer is, it almost didn't. A comet struck the Yucatán Peninsula in the late Jurassic period and exterminated all land animals larger than your fist. Nevertheless, such cataclysms have been rare enough to let Earth thrive. The reason for that lies closer in; we tighten our focus, cropping out Pluto, and find the Jovian planets standing guard over our city.

The Jovian planets are tremendously massive. Jupiter, in particular, is so heavy that it would, if otherwise situated, be called a star. The vital role of Jupiter in shielding New York lies in this very massiveness. Jupiter sweeps through the solar system like a vacuum cleaner, denuding it of countless hazards. Comets and asteroids fall into the planet constantly, yielding their mass to it. In 1996, one particularly spectacular suicide was visible to astronomers, as the Shoemaker-Levy comet smashed into Jupiter's eye. If that comet had reached Earth, the explosion would have sterilized our planet forever. Jupiter ran interference and still wears the scars today.

Zooming in tighter on New York, we narrow our focus again. The asteroid belt drops out of view, then Mars. Finally we see a spark in the void; the planet we at Jinx call the Greater New York Area.

EARTH, JULY 16, 1609

It appears, as Carl Sagan described it, "a mote of dust suspended in a sunbeam."

This view of Earth seems to confirm what every person has felt, staring up from the countryside into the heavenly firmament. Seeing the Earth as a mere pixel against the yawning hugeness of space drags us below humility. The universe's infinity, and our pitiful share of it, is the beginning of man's sense of insignificance.

Relativity offers a road up from the infinitesimal. The measure of value, like all measures, must depend on perspective. So we ask, as our lens brings Earth more sharply into view, where does the importance truly lie? Where will we turn for meaning, in this Local Group of galaxies? Where is all the action in the Milky Way? Even in the solar system, is there great significance to be found in the emptiness beyond Pluto?

To the best of our knowledge, the whole night sky above Earth is empty and lifeless. In the whole age of the universe, the limitless void of space could never produce the life in one drop of pond water. If there are other inhabited worlds out there, we should gladly acknowledge their importance. But as for the cold blackness of interstellar space, its significance comes from here, this tiny planet, where eyes first opened to see it. The whole ocean of space is not so precious as the tiny gem floating through it.

This is an urban perspective, of course. The city-dweller never worries that the vast countryside could diminish his home. The city is small, compared to the rivers and oceans and fields that surround it. But the city isn't humbled. In the urban perspective, the world is a mere backdrop.

By now that world reveals vivid detail. We can see the edges of the oceans, and the land is set off in relief. The East Coast of North America can be discerned. Snug against that coast is a hub, the axis of the wheel of space.

NEW YORK STATE, JULY 16, 1609

It's not called New York State yet. This is pastoral country, rich in greenery, ridged with mountains and pocked with shining lakes. Local Indian tribes, such as Hurons, Montagnais, and Algonquins wander across this territory. They hunt, they fish, and they grow simple crops to supplement their diets.

The past winter has been brutally fierce. The local tribes, facing starvation, have set out to the south, into Iroquois country, to find fresh game. We see them now in their canoes, heading into the unknown. But this is no ordinary hunting expedition, for among them is Samuel de Champlain.

Champlain is Royal Geographer of France, founder of Quebec City, his country's greatest explorer since Giovanni de Verrazano sailed under the French flag. Champlain's most fruitful years began in 1603, when he landed in Canada. He smoked the peace pipe there with the local tribes and began to establish settlements. By 1605, Champlain had founded Port Royal, the Acadie settlement. (Many of these Acadians would soon flee for Louisiana, where their name was bastardized into "Cajuns.") In 1608, Champlain put down a rebellion by some Basque smugglers; they were colluding with his own settlers. Champlain called the traitors to the bar, holding the first-ever trial in North America. One of the guilty was hanged, and his head was impaled on a pike.

At this moment Champlain rides down into the lake in a canoe. His party consists of sixty Indians and two other Frenchmen. War is imminent. As a pledge of his friendship to the Hurons and Algonquins, Champlain has promised to fight any Iroquois they find. That day is just fifteen days off, and the battle they fight will begin one and a half centuries of French-Iroquois enmity. For now, though, he and his party are exploring. He will record it in his journal:

> [We] entered the lake. Continuing our way along this lake in a westerly direction and viewing the country, I saw towards the east very high mountains on the tops of which there was snow. I inquired of the natives whether these parts were inhabited. They said they were, and by the Iroquois, and that in those parts there were beautiful valleys and fields rich in corn such as I have eaten in that country, along with other products in abundance. And they said that the lake went close to the mountains, which, as I judged, might be some twenty-five leagues away from us. Towards the south I saw others which were not less lofty than the first-mentioned, but there was no snow on these. The Indians told me that it was there that we were to meet their enemies, that the mountains were thickly populated, and that we had to pass a rapid which I saw afterwards. . . .

This is a greater sight than he realizes. The lake over which he drifts will bear his name. And entering the beautiful valleys and rich fields ahead, with their corn and other products in abundance, he will today discover New York State.

Now, instead of zooming in, we pan to the south. Just four hundred miles and nine weeks from this spot, another great discovery is under way.

NEW YORK, NEW YORK, SEPTEMBER 12, 1609

Across the mirrored surface of New York Harbor, the *Half Moon* glides slowly along the Manhattan shore. She is a Dutch East India Company vessel, out of Amsterdam. Her captain is Henry Hudson. For ten days, he has explored this harbor, which Verrazano before him described as "a very pleasant situation amongst some steep hills." Verrazano, discovering the harbor back in 1524, had also noted a "Grand River," but had not gone up it.

The *Half-Moon*'s survey has confirmed Verrazano's eighty-five-year-old description. Hudson agrees it is a pleasant situation, but does not realize it will be the busiest harbor in North America. He has come to find a northern route through the Americas, so that ships won't have to round the Cape of Good Hope to reach the Orient. He looks at this "Grand River," noting its wide draught. This river will be named for him. He gives the order to sail.

When Hudson returns to the Old World, he will tell his company about the new river, the harbor, and especially the island that separates them, "as pleasant a land as one can tread upon." Others will soon follow, and a Dutch colony on Manhattan will be founded in fifteen years.

Today they cautiously tack along Manhattan's western shore, gazing over the rough country. Hudson notes a narrow channel toward the north end of the island, where the cliffs on both sides are closest together. He glances at a two-hundred-thirty-foot cliff on the Manhattan side of the river. As he sails further north, we will remain here. On this same cliff, one hundred sixty-eight years later, patriots not yet born will stand their ground for a country not yet dreamed of.

FORT WASHINGTON, NEW YORK, NOVEMBER 16, 1776

New York is in flames. A British expeditionary force has attacked in the navy's largest amphibious landing before D-Day. Patriots have been beaten back from Brooklyn to Kip's Bay, in the most important strategic retreat since ancient Rome. The army has been driven up to Murray Hill, then routed again at Harlem. Retreating to White Plains, General Washington has reluctantly left a garrison on this cliff around a fortress. Fort Washington commands the river, overlooking it here at the narrowest stretch. Despite this strategic value Washington has vainly argued that the fort be abandoned; he is convinced it will be taken.

This is the day. The British forces, both Hessian and British battalions, cross the Hudson and Harlem Rivers to Manhattan. The enemy attacks the near-vertical cliffs, singing war songs as they encircle the patriots. A British naval attachment from the Harlem River heads in to cut off retreat. Many Americans have been caught outside the fort and must fight their way back.

As it will be reported in *The Freeman's Journal* or *New-Hampshire Gazette,*

[Our] small army under the command of Col. Magaw, retreated, sustaining with unexampled resolution, a contin-

**ual fire of the cannon, field pieces and musketry of more
than five to one in number.**

The battle is a rout. The fort will fall, and with it precious arms and munitions. Fifty-three Americans will die fighting here today. The survivors will be sent to British prison ships, where many more will succumb to atrocious conditions there. No American here today will be more honored for valor than Margaret Cochran Corbin, also known as "Captain Molly."

When Margaret Corbin was five, Indians raided her farm, killing her father and carrying off her mother. Years later, when the war came, Margaret's husband John enlisted in the patriot army. This time she would not be left behind. She became a camp follower in her husband's unit. Along with the other wives, she did laundry and cleaning for the soldiers. Unlike the other wives, "Moll" liked to join in the artillery drills, learning to charge and load the cannons, even to fire them.

Now we see her at the battle line below Fort Washington. The enemy is converging from all sides, outnumbering the defenders almost three to one. The Hessians are bayoneting Americans who try to surrender.

Margaret assists her husband John with his cannon. A barrage of grapeshot rips through the camp, shattering the line and killing John almost instantly. After a moment with her fallen spouse, Molly takes up the rammer. She proceeds to man the cannon and return the enemy fire. By the time the British overrun Fort Washington, Molly will be shot twice; the second shot nearly severing her left arm. She will never raise that arm again.

In 1779 Captain Molly Corbin will be awarded a disabled soldier's pension by the Continental Congress and in 1780 will become the only woman enrolled in the "Invalid Regiment." When she eventually dies, the United States Army will bury her in the soldier's graveyard at West Point with a bronze plaque that reads, "the first American woman to take a soldier's part in the War for Liberty."

Molly's is not the only memorial from this siege. America makes another dedication on this battleground, fifty-six thousand, five hundred thirty-four days later.

GEORGE WASHINGTON BRIDGE, NEW YORK, OCTOBER 25, 1931

On this cliff, which three thousand fought to defend, thirty thousand now gather to open the George Washington Bridge. None of them has seen anything like it before. More than anything, the new bridge amazes by its enormity. Its span reaches almost three-quarters of a mile, more than twice the length of the world's next-longest suspension bridge. For towers, the bridge has two skyscrapers, two of the tallest in the city, each more than six hundred feet high. The crowd is used to flat granite fronts, as the Brooklyn Bridge has, but the George Washington presents an open frame of exposed steel latticework. Sunshine streams through. Each of its four suspension cables, they learn, weighs twenty-eight thousand tons.

When engineers dream, they dream of bridges. Today, at its opening, the George Washington Bridge fulfills the dreams of three generations. Sought for over a century, the bridge has taken just four years to build. The Depression is on, but this is not a Federal Relief project. Free enterprise has powered the construction from the start. The Port Authority selected Othmar Ammann as the chief engineer, because his design was best. Ammann chose Roebling & Sons to assemble the wire suspension because they were the best bargain. New York's first ever professional bridge crew was assembled for the construction; that crew was divided into competing teams, each racing to finish its section first. The bridge has cost twelve lives and sixty million dollars, but now it's done, six months ahead of schedule.

Dozens of elected officials from New York and New Jersey stand now on the dais, overlooking the crowd. The radio stations are broadcasting every sound. A speaker moves to the microphones and unfolds a speech. He will dedicate this bridge to America's first great wartime leader. What no one here knows is that the speaker himself is about to become America's next great wartime leader. Governor Franklin D. Roosevelt of New York tells the crowd,

In every patriotic sanctuary, there is at least one figure so serenely certain of enduring honor that the scrutiny of centuries can never shake its permanence. In dedicating the George Washington Bridge, we pay tribute not so much to the military triumphs of a great general, not to the attainments of a great executive, but to a more precious heritage. We offer homage to great ideals, exemplified in Washington's career and stamped indelibly upon our national thought.

Out of the wealth of vital principles demonstrated by his deeds, I feel that three are peculiarly significant and especially appropriate to this occasion. They are the worth of integrity, the need for intelligence and the fact of our independence.

It should be an inspiration to us to recall that here, at Fort Washington in 1776, our forebears made one of the most valiant stands against insurmountable obstacles of the entire Revolutionary War. Here, at Jeffrey's Hook, Washington and his generals once struggled to block this channel against a hostile fleet with the sunken hulls of ships. Here, in a defense unmatched for heroism, 3,000 Americans sacrificed all for a great cause. We may rejoice that this great bridge marks a site so sacred in patriotic memories.

We leave this great speaker and this great speech, moving from the sublime to the ridiculous: just overhead, seventy years later.

GEORGE WASHINGTON BRIDGE, ALTITUDE 320 FEET, SEPTEMBER 9, 2001, 7:45 P.M.

The George Washington Bridge over the Hudson is the most beautiful bridge in the world. Made of cables and steel beams, it gleams in the sky like a reversed arch. It is blessed. It is the only seat of grace in the disordered city. It is painted an aluminum color and, between water and sky, you see nothing but the bent cord supported by two steel towers. When your car moves up the ramp, the two towers rise so high that it brings you happiness; their structure is so pure, so resolute, so regular that here, finally, steel architecture seems to laugh. . . . The second tower is very far away; innumerable vertical cables, gleaming across the sky, are suspended from the magisterial curve that swings down and then up. The rose-colored towers of New York appear, a vision whose harshness is mitigated by distance.

Le Corbusier

I cling to the open lattices of the Manhattan tower, climbing with Illich and Duncan toward the top. The sun is setting, and the New Jersey tower in the distance has softened to a fiery haze. Though high above the river, we are just starting out; we have just left Renée, Mike, Josh, and Lefty on the pedestrian walkway. They're sixty feet below me now, waiting for us, watching out for the authorities.

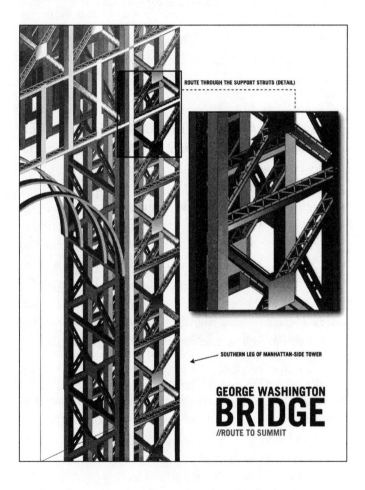

ROUTE THROUGH THE SUPPORT STRUTS (DETAIL)

SOUTHERN LEG OF MANHATTAN-SIDE TOWER

GEORGE WASHINGTON
BRIDGE
//ROUTE TO SUMMIT

The tower wasn't designed to be climbed. Most New York bridges have some maintenance ladders or stairs leading to the top, but here is only a locked elevator. The bridge is simply too large for ladders. The tower has three main sections; two are the legs, one on each side of the causeway that threads between them. The third part is the tower's upper canopy, bridging the two legs of the tower in a closed arch. There will be stairs in the canopy, and floors; the canopy is roughly fifteen stories high. For now, though, we're climbing girders.

The girders that crisscross up the sides of these towers are built like long coffins, each some sixty-five feet in length. The sides are closed, but the tops and bottoms are open, crosshatched with small metal slats. The structure of these girders allows us to climb. We can use these slats as handholds, scaling up along a forty-five-degree angle. Then we can slide between the slats to move through the girders, sometimes passing to a higher girder, sometimes continuing to climb while inside the girder itself.

It's sweaty work. If the exertion isn't bad enough (imagine crawling up fifty flights of stairs in a suit and tie) the view can shake you up. Climbing in an open structure is close to flying; the drop is unobstructed. On the outside of the tower is a drop to the walkway, on the inside you can see all the way to the tower's base in the river. I pull myself up and out of a girder, and stop to rest on top.

"How you doing?" I shout to Illich, just below me. This is Illich's first mission. He's been at sea most of the summer and missed most of the operation. I hope he has his land legs back.

He looks up as though startled. His face glows with sweat. "I don't know," he says. "I'm feeling pretty *exposed* up here."

I see what he means. There's a family down on the walkway, about two hundred feet from Lefty and his team. The family isn't moving. Are they pointing at us, the busybodies? "Mind your business," I sneer. Have they never seen well-dressed men climb a bridge before? Goddamn their eyes!

GEORGE WASHINGTON BRIDGE, ALTITUDE 490 FEET, SEPTEMBER 9, 2001, 9:45 P.M.

New Jersey snuffs out the last rays of sunlight as we reach the upper canopy. The situation is not good. A floor, which workers can step out onto from the elevator, is to us a ceiling. We can't climb these girders any higher.

The bridge has come alive with thousands of blue-white halogen lights. They filter through the latticework, casting deceptive shadows across the steel.

"What do you think?" I shout to Duncan and Illich.

Duncan removes his sunglasses and studies the tower around us. "I see stairs over there." He points through a dense mesh of girders, pipes, and steel plates at the canopy interior. There are catwalks inside, with guardrails and other lavish amenities. "I think we're going to have to sort of squeeze through this opening."

It's no sooner said than done, for that skinny bastard. Somehow Illich squeezes his way through, too.

"*Bastards!*" I hiss, straining against the opening. It's like trying to strain through the closed doors of an elevator. "Not even close. I can't fit."

I tell the two slender gentlemen to proceed for the summit. If I can find another way into the canopy, I'll catch up with them.

So now I'm alone in the darkness, forty stories in the sky, gripping the metal slats of a semi-horizontal girder. I have two choices. The first is to give up, wait here while my two compatriots conquer the bridge, then climb down and explain that I was too "husky" to join them. The other choice is to step off the girder onto the vertical tower wall, climb around to the side, and look for another way in.

This is a strange paradise. The sky around me is so empty.

When this operation began four months ago, we took on the Old Aqueduct with a team of seven. With each mission since then, our team has gotten smaller. Agents dropped out in ones and twos, always for the best of reasons, as we wended our way through the depths of the city up to its surface, and then upward into the heights of New York. Now I'm grabbing hold of the steel, gently lifting one foot off the girder and placing it in a foothold of the tower wall. A deep breath, and I bring my other foot over. There are just two men up here with me. Why? Some team members may have departed because of the risks; it would be foolish to ignore the self-preservation instinct. But our greatest enemy has been our oldest: everyday life. Bills have to be paid, phone calls must be returned. Work takes so much out of you that most days you don't consider anything but heading home to relax. Whatever our aversion to heat, discomfort, high precipices, and live third rails, nothing argues against exploration like a warm couch, a remote control. The real enemy of adventure is eighty-five television channels.

I climb to the outside of the tower structure, hanging on as though to the face of a skyscraper. My back is now to the span of the bridge. I have to look down; it's the only way to see footholds. So I see it: the big nothing. Forty stories of empty space, terminated by the black waters of the Hudson. It would take half a minute to fall. At moments like this I like to close my eyes, inhale, and feel the cold of the steel in my grip.

This is the panic threshold. My breathing goes fast and shallow. My heart hammers into my rib cage. Dopamine, adrenaline, and noradrenaline pulse through me. Behind the shades, my pupils have dilated. The sympathetic nervous system diverts blood flow to my skeletal muscles, away from other organs: The stomach cramps up, the skin cools and itches, the eyes see spots, and the head goes light and dizzy.

Stronger than all these physical symptoms are the psychological effects. Confusion and unreality take hold. My body feels alien, as though my hands and feet no longer exist. I see the tower stretch down below me, twisting in a hallucinatory warp.

Yet nature weds a paradoxical benefit to this wash of fear. The mind, buffeted by terror, narrows and sharpens its focus. Irrelevancies, abstractions, the past and the future blur to the edges. At the center remains the moment in its essential data of survival: the immediate environment, my state of readiness, the threat, available means of escape. These details, normally overlooked, burn into my brain.

If urban exploration is worth anything, this is why. In the diamond clarity of fear we find the difference between speculation and experience, between philosophy and science. It's the difference between reading about the George Washington Bridge and climbing it.

On the outside of the tower I find a gap I can squeeze through. Barely able to see, I slip through a knot of metal into the canopy interior. In the darkness, I find a catwalk and grab hold of a railing, doubled over for air. The floor feels as solid as bedrock. A staircase will bring me up the rest of the way to the top of the bridge. I take out a hand-kerchief and wipe the sweat from my eyes, my forehead, my neck, and my sunglasses. It's time to join Duncan and Illich. Though I don't yet know it, the operation is in its final hour.

GEORGE WASHINGTON BRIDGE, ALTITUDE 220 FEET, SEPTEMBER 9, 2001, 9:55 P.M.

As I link up with Illich and Duncan in the upper floors of the canopy, we are oblivious to the danger unfolding hundreds of feet below. (We'll hear about it only on returning to the main span.)

The police are here. In the failing light, no one has spotted them walking from the Manhattan shore. Then Renée turns and says, "Cops."

Lefty, Mike, Josh, and Renée slump into casual mode simultaneously, leaning against the rail, pointing into the distance, whistling.

"How are you folks tonight?" the first officer says. He and his partner are in casual mode too.

Everybody's fine, great, never better.

"You see anybody acting funny out here?" the second officer asks, tapping a pen against his notebook.

"No, hell no," Josh jumps in after a pause. "No, sir. We're up here from North Carolina for the weekend, and we wanted to get a look at the sunset from the bridge. It was pretty spectacular. See, I got my camera. Took some beautiful shots. Fantastic."

The cops give Josh a little ice-water stare, then turn to Renée.

"We got a call there might be some bungee jumpers out here," says the first one.

"Maybe they saw your backpacks and got the wrong idea," says the second.

"That's probably what happened." Josh laughs. "You know how people get all kinds of crazy ideas. We sure would have noticed if anybody had been bungee jumping, though. We've been out here about two hours."

The cops wish everyone a good evening and head back toward Manhattan.

"What do you think?" Lefty asks the group. "They buy it?"

Josh smiles, and nods his head. "No way."

GEORGE WASHINGTON BRIDGE, ALTITUDE 601 FEET, SEPTEMBER 9, 2001, 10:10 P.M.

What can ever be more stately and admirable to me than mast-hemm'd Manhattan?

Walt Whitman, "Crossing Brooklyn Ferry"

We're at the highest point of the bridge. It's quite a bit more than we expected. The tower roof is awash in red aircraft warning lights. A radar dish, mounted on the northeast corner, whirls rapidly through the night air. Illich and Duncan move ecstatically around the highest ledge, peering down over Manhattan, letting the adrenaline and wind rush over them.

Standing six hundred feet up on a hundred thousand tons of steel, we look out into the night sky and see a second galaxy spread out at our feet, reflecting back the heavens. This frontier is small and fragile but alive: a complex system of complex systems, pulsing with small infinities. Our city, unplanned and untamed since its earliest origins, always like a loose turbine threatening to spin out of control; a city hovering, as all hives do, between order and chaos, never drifting far enough toward either extreme to die, but just enough to adapt and evolve. A city of kinetic drive frozen in soaring glacial monuments and labyrinthine depths. A city always stretching farther, with new roots and new branches, into the air, the earth, and other dimensions too: politics and commerce, art and culture, education, crime, the struggle of science and progress against disease and poverty, the ebb and flow of eight million human lives. Looking out now into its democratic vistas, drunk with altitude, we permit ourselves a claim of success: We have discovered a city. We have found New York.

THE MID-FIRMAMENT

> With the coming forward of Greece, mankind became the center of the universe, the most important thing in it. This was a revolution in thought. Human beings had counted for little heretofore. In Greece man first realized what man was.
>
> **Edith Hamilton,** *Mythology*

The fifth century B.C. was a dark age. In Europe and Africa, tribal savagery prevailed; illiterate hunter-gatherer bands roamed, fighting starvation and one another. In the Near East, ancient kingdoms that had long since declined into decadence luxuriated in cruelty and superstition. The light that rose from this sea of barbarism and tyranny was Athens. It would be a model for the world.

Fifth-century Athens has been described as a miracle. It was the greatest concentration of intellect in human history. Philosophy, geometry, tragic poetry, empirical science, the discipline of history, and democracy all were born in the Athens streets at a time when most of humanity still slept in caves. It wasn't a miracle, exactly. It was just a free city, the first free city. Foreigners came to trade, creating a cosmopolitan culture. Citizens not only voted but lived under the rule of law. It was a marketplace where ideas competed and cultures were refined. The freedom and prosperity gave Athenians leisure to consider abstract things, instead of worrying about offending a king or starving in the winter. Among these Athenians were Socrates, Aristotle, Diogenes, Thucydides, Plato, Thales, Empedocles, Sophocles, Aristophanes, and Alexander the Great, who conquered Persia and began the advance of Hellenic culture across the world.

Twenty-five centuries later, the cycle has reversed. The light that spread from Athens is in full retreat. In the free world, humanist institutions are failing fast. The universities, once monuments to moral and intellectual education, are now mostly sleep-away camps where spoiled children learn treason, conspiracy theories, superstition, and soft thinking.

For most of the planet, the situation is far worse. Just as in Plato's time, the great mass of humanity slaves under despotism: socialist totalitarian states, as in China, Cuba, North Korea, and much of Asia and Africa; theocratic monarchies, as in most of the Middle East; or other corrupt dictatorships. Whole continents suffer poverty, privation, disease, starvation, and ignorance, with their own governments the main source of the misery. Millions of people share a single dream: to escape with their families to peace, prosperity, and freedom. Once again, the world looks to a pocket of light.

In 431 B.C., Athens was at war, fighting for its survival against the Peloponnesian city-states. In an oration at the funeral of several fallen Athenian soldiers, Pericles celebrated their courage and reminded the citizens how fortunate they were to live in freedom, cosmopolitanism, and the rule of law. His praise glorifies Athens, but not only Athens. He is also describing another pocket of light across the sea of time.

> If we look to the laws, they afford equal justice to all within their private differences; if to social standing, advancement in public life falls to reputation for capacity, class considerations not being allowed to interfere with merit. . . . The freedom which we enjoy in our government extends also to ordinary life. There, far from exercising a jealous surveillance over each other, we do not feel called upon to be angry with our neighbor for doing what he likes.
>
> We throw open our city to the world, and never by alien acts exclude foreigners from any opportunity of learning or observing, although the eyes of an enemy may occasionally profit by our liberality; trusting less in system and policy than in the native spirit of our citizens; while in education, where our rivals from their very cradles by a painful discipline seek after manliness, at Athens we live exactly as we please, and yet are just as ready to encounter every legitimate danger.

It's ten-thirty P.M. None of us feels the slightest premonition that in thirty-six hours, at 9:06 A.M. September 11, 2001, an enemy will profit by our liberality. The darkness of the outer world will punch through.

Renée, Lefty, Mike, and Josh have waited for hours on the deck of the bridge. Duncan, Illich, and I must now cautiously make our way down the girders to join them. We'll go home tonight to bed and go back to work on

Monday, and as we lead our lives we'll try to retain some image of our present discovery.

I take a last look down the main cables, four rows of lights trailing back to earth, and out over the dark river, following it down to the horizon's electric glow. This bridge is such a sublime vantage, with its cold steel framework and harsh glare, a snowy Olympus over New York.

PHOTOGRAPH CREDITS

INDEX